Praise for *Like a Child*

"This highly readable book is a helpful reminder that one of the most radical, and important, things Jesus said was 'become like children.' Tim Mooney, with a scholar's careful eye and a pastor's heart, explores the meanings of Jesus' words and all the reasons the adult demands of modernity mitigate against them. In the process he employs the insights of art, theology, literature, popular culture and his own winsome humanity to invite us to become the children Jesus meant. This is an important book."
—**John Buchanan**, editor/publisher, *The Christian Century*

"If we grown-ups would only heed the beautifully written yet immensely practical wisdom in this jewel of a book, we can rediscover the ability to give ourselves wholeheartedly to all aspects of life and, even in the dark times, fully embrace joy and wonder as God's beloved children. What better way to live?"
—**The Rev. Peter Wallace**, *Day1* radio host; author, *The Passionate Jesus: What We Can Learn from Jesus about Love, Fear, Grief, Joy and Living Authentically*

"Who of us has not wondered, and argued with ourselves, about why Jesus praised spiritual childhood so much? What did he mean by that? This might be the most intelligent, inspiring, and integrated book I have read on the subject. Tim Mooney will not give you clichés or glib answers here, but genuine wisdom."
—**Richard Rohr**, OFM, Center for Action and Contemplation, Albuquerque, NM

"Tim Mooney offers us the vital gift of learning to take ourselves less seriously. In this delightful exploration of what it really means to bring a childlike trust and joy to daily life, we are called to a sweet lightness of being. Those seeking a new way forward into their spiritual practice will find much nourishment for the soul."
—**Christine Valters Paintner, PhD**, author, *Lectio Divina—The Sacred Art Transforming Words & Images into Hea*

D1040536

"When you do an online search of the word 'childlike,' the first association is 'childlike faith.' *Like a Child* is a book about faith, for its author, like Jesus, invites us to become like children and boldly explore the realm of grace. A seasoned pastor and spiritual director, Timothy Mooney proves a trustworthy guide on this adventure, equipping the reader with navigational aids in the form of biblical understandings, spiritual practices, and stories from those who've undertaken the journey. This book inspires hope ... and faith."

—**Susan S. Phillips, PhD**, sociologist and spiritual director; executive director and Christian studies professor at New College Berkeley; author, *Candlelight: Illuminating the Art of Spiritual Direction*

"Helps us recover one of the most transforming treasures of Jesus—the secret to growing up without growing old. With the sensitivity of a spiritual director, the practicality of a pastor, and the colorful brush of an artist, Tim Mooney leads us into the splendor of a childlike maturity."

—**Dr. Daniel Meyer**, senior pastor, Christ Church of Oak Brook; host, Life Focus Television

LIKE A
Child

RESTORING THE AWE, WONDER, JOY
& RESILIENCY OF THE HUMAN SPIRIT

REV. TIMOTHY J. MOONEY

CHRISTIAN JOURNEYS
FROM SKYLIGHT PATHS® PUBLISHING
Woodstock, Vermont

Like a Child:
Restoring the Awe, Wonder, Joy & Resiliency of the Human Spirit
2014 Quality Paperback Edition, First Printing
© 2014 by Timothy J. Mooney

For information regarding permission to reprint material from this book, please mail or fax your request in writing to SkyLight Paths Publishing, Permissions Department, at the address / fax number listed below, or email your request to permissions@skylightpaths.com.

Library of Congress Cataloging-in-Publication Data
Mooney, Timothy J., 1957–
Like a child : restoring the awe, wonder, joy and resiliency of the human spirit / Rev. Timothy J. Mooney.
pages cm
Includes bibliographical references.
ISBN 978-1-59473-543-1 (quality pbk.) — ISBN 978-1-59473-570-7 (ebook) 1. Spiritual life—Christianity. 2. Spirituality—Christianity. 3. Spiritual formation. I. Title.
BV4501.3.M6525 2014
248.4—dc23
                                    2014009303

10 9 8 7 6 5 4 3 2 1

Manufactured in the United States of America
Cover design: Jenny Buono
Cover art: © micro10x / Shutterstock
Interior design: Tim Holtz

SkyLight Paths Publishing is creating a place where people of different spiritual traditions come together for challenge and inspiration, a place where we can help each other understand the mystery that lies at the heart of our existence.

SkyLight Paths sees both believers and seekers as a community that increasingly transcends traditional boundaries of religion and denomination—people wanting to learn from each other, *walking together, finding the way®*.

SkyLight Paths, "Walking Together, Finding the Way" and colophon are trademarks of LongHill Partners, Inc., registered in the U.S. Patent and Trademark Office.

Walking Together, Finding the Way®
Published by SkyLight Paths Publishing
A Division of LongHill Partners, Inc.
Sunset Farm Offices, Route 4, P.O. Box 237
Woodstock, VT 05091
Tel: (802) 457-4000   Fax: (802) 457-4004
www.skylightpaths.com

Contents

Introduction

Unless you change and become like children
you will never enter the kingdom of heaven.

JESUS (MATTHEW 18:3)

It takes a long time to become young.

PABLO PICASSO

G row up, mature, leave behind childish things, and become responsible people of faith. This is what the Apostle Paul exhorts his readers
to pursue as the spiritual task of life. He says:

> We must no longer be children, tossed to and fro and blown about
> by every wind of doctrine, by people's trickery, by their craftiness
> in deceitful scheming. But speaking the truth in love, we must
> grow up in every way into him who is the head, into Christ.
> (Ephesians 4:14–15)

Paul seemingly did just that, as he described in 1 Corinthians 13:11:
"When I was a child I spoke like a child, I thought like a child, I reasoned
like a child; when I became an adult I put an end to childish ways."

How odd it is, then, to hear these words of Jesus: "Unless you change
and become like children, you will never enter the kingdom of heaven."
This is one of the few sayings of Jesus that has not been explored to any
great extent. Much has been made of healing the inner child in therapeutic
circles, but few therapists have explored the meaning and development of
childlike qualities in adulthood. In a culture that many would characterize
as selfish, narcissistic, and childish, this book serves as a way to—sorry,

I just can't resist the joke—not throw the baby out with the bathwater. It aims to address misconceptions regarding the nature of maturity, adulthood, and spiritual growth, and recover a fuller picture of what it means to be human.

I once preached a series of sermons titled *Like a Child*, and that launched me on a fascinating exploration of the implications of what Jesus's words might mean for us individually and communally. I shared with my congregation that children are childlike naturally, without effort or forethought. They cannot help but be childlike because it is who they are.

How, then, are we to become childlike? Why is becoming childlike so important for our spiritual lives? What kinds of changes are needed for us to become like children? What must we do to cultivate the necessary changes? And why, as Pablo Picasso suggests, would it take such a long time?

I have been a pastor for twenty-five years, and a spiritual director, staff member, and adjunct professor in the program leading to a diploma in the Art of Spiritual Direction at San Francisco Theological Seminary for almost fifteen years. In my ministry and spiritual direction practice, I have seen how childlike qualities emerge as individuals gain increasing self-awareness and embrace spiritual practices. I have also observed how these qualities play a prominent role in spiritual growth, maturity, and discernment. I have witnessed congregants practicing a serious, somber approach to faith to their detriment, and I have watched parishioners with a sense of wonder about God and life, a sense of playfulness, and the ability to laugh at themselves become spiritual leaders and harbingers of grace. In my own personal life as an artist, musician, and writer, I have found that the more I am able to play at my crafts and vocations, the more creative and productive I become.

My own spiritual path has been greatly affected by an initial denial and eventual (lengthy) reclamation of childlike qualities. I grew up in a conservative tradition that expected adult behavior out of children, and it's been a long and at times difficult road of reclaiming the fullness of my humanity, much of it rooted in childlike qualities. I hope this book—the culmination of personal and professional exploration and experiment—becomes a helpful resource for the cultivation of childlike qualities in your life and the spiritual fulfillment that it can bring you.

Spiritual Transformation: An Adventure

Spiritual transformation calls for change, a fundamental resetting of our perspective, orientation, and vision. It also calls for an accompanying change in the behaviors that shape our lives and our world. Our goal here is to reintroduce ourselves to childlike (not childish) behaviors and attitudes that can liberate our soul from the confines of ego-driven false selfhood. But *how* are we to effect these changes? *brothers*

In an age of specialization and expertise, we tend to depend on experts for wisdom and guidance. Conversely, in a postmodern world suspicious of authority and meta-stories, we want to value our own experiences. The practices in this book invite you to experience for yourself what it might mean to become like a child. Much of what Jesus taught, and how he taught, came from observing nature, from seeing what there is to see. He invited his followers into a deeper awareness of life itself. This book invites you to deeply explore the qualities that you observe in children—and once exhibited yourself, when you were a child—and then to find and experience them in your adult life.

We begin the adventure by revisiting childlike trust—the ability to wholeheartedly give ourselves over to all aspects of life. We start here because we enable spiritual growth when we live more fully from the heart. With this understanding, we set out to reclaim childlike humility, putting pride and shame aside in favor of a self-image aligned with reality. Restoring our capacity for wonder and our innocent eyes are next up: How else will we recognize the great "I Am" burning all around us and be able to discern what we see in ourselves and others as God does? We then reinterpret our tantrum-like expressions as a way to communicate the unlived parts of our true self. When we willingly (not willfully) embrace these deep longings, we begin to see how we might manifest our desires without fear, and so become whole.

Our spiritual path continues when we aim to use "beginner's mind" to break out of spiritual, mental, and physical ruts and into the fullness of life. We can't leave behind our habitual ways of doing, thinking, and feeling successfully until we tackle the practice of forgiveness, which is so difficult for adults but seemingly easy for children. We then seek to recover the body-mind-spirit connection by seeing our bodies not as targets of denigration and demonization but as sources of wisdom and truth. What better way to celebrate the body than to laugh and play, to not take ourselves so seriously and to honor the outlandishness of God's grace? When children play, they are exercising their imagination and their capacity to dream. We can do the same.

In the final steps along our journey we are invited to drop our shields, come out from behind the walls we build to hide our true self, and accept ourselves for the gloriously flawed, divinely created beings we are. By doing this, we pave the way for our spiritual rebirthing, in which our soul emerges free of the molds, impressions, and assumptions we accumulated in our quest for so-called maturity. Children are not burdened by their God-given strangeness and beauty. Only when we as embrace our strangeness and beauty will we fully know the essence of our soul.

Not all of what we will encounter in this book will come easily, comfortably, or quickly. Becoming like a child is a lifelong journey. What we have come to know as the path of maturity and adulthood is deeply ingrained in our psyche. But we were all children once—regardless of our faith background and upbringing—and therefore we have what it takes to embark on and benefit from this new spiritual adventure.

The Kingdom of Heaven: Here and Now

In my understanding of Jesus's words, becoming like a child is a way to enter the realm of grace (what Jesus called the kingdom of heaven or the kingdom of God) in the here and now, in all its ways of being and seeing, its attitudes and actions. We achieve this by embracing the childlike qualities of attention, self-awareness, and practice, and the experience of living into the reality of right relationships governed by love, acceptance, grace, and justice.

"Unless you change and become like children, you will never enter the kingdom of heaven." Jesus said these words to peasants and disciples, to people like you and me, who have one key characteristic in common—we were once children. The invitation is for us to choose to become childlike once again—an essential element for entering God's realm of love and light.

1 Cowabunga!

RESTING IN WHOLEHEARTED TRUST

Trust is the basis of life. Without trust,
no human being can live.
HENRI NOUWEN

Have enough courage to trust love one
more time and always one more time.
MAYA ANGELOU

I asked my congregation one Sunday morning, "What do you think it means to become like a child?" Once my congregation realized I was actually inviting them to respond out loud and publicly, a rare if not unheard-of request during a sermon, the silence erupted with voices:

Inexperienced

Little

Vulnerable

Uninhibited ✓

Free

Spontaneous ✓

Independent and
dependent

Innocent ✓

Trusting ✓

Hopeful

Optimistic

Humorous

Full of laughter ✓

Forthrightly tactful

Throwing tantrums

1

Whiny   In the moment ✓

Stubborn ✓   Awe-filled ✓

Present ✓

Quite a list, and suddenly all of us were surprised by the breadth and depth of what it might mean to become like a child. But when we whittled it down, we discovered that the essence of becoming childlike meant having childlike trust.

Trust: Take a Seat

Trust is a common word in our vocabulary and an essential element for our relationships with self, others, institutions, society, and the world. But what is trust? Is there a difference between childlike trust and the kind of trust we usually engage in as adults?

In an online dictionary, the first five definitions of *trust* treat it as a noun. But *trust*, at its root, is a verb. It is something we do. The online definitions of *trust* as a verb read, "to have confidence in, to rely or depend on; to believe; to expect confidently; to hope." But these definitions lack something. They do not convey the complexity and nuance of the concept, the difficulty we have in offering our trust, and the challenge of earning and keeping the trust of others. And yet trust must be exercised if we are to learn anything about ourselves and the world around us.

Recently, I was asked to speak to a Scout troop about God, and the conversation centered on finding the meaning of *trust* and *faith*. I asked the Scouts, seated in folding chairs in front of me, what they thought *faith* meant. Several boys said, "Trust." I asked them what *trust* meant and they said, "Faith, faith in God." The circular pattern of their attempts to define these two words revealed the challenge of getting to the bottom of these concepts. I thought it might be easier to focus on trust.

"All of you are trusting in something this very second." I asked, "Do you know what it is?"

Blank stares. Then one Scout shot his hand into the air and said cautiously, "Our chairs?"

Blank stares turned into lightbulbs when the Scouts suddenly realized they knew what trust felt like in their bodies. And it's true. We easily fall into chairs with our full weight, without hesitation, repeatedly throughout the day. Once seated, we may notice whether a chair is uncomfortable or perhaps not fully balanced, but rarely, if ever, do we stop to question the stability and strength of the chair, or its ability to continually support us.

After the Scouts realized how completely they trusted the chairs in which they sat, I asked them to show me what it would be like not to have trust in their chairs. I was treated to a comical and exhausting display of teetering anxiety and worry—a powerful metaphor for the way we often experience our lives. We are doubtful, worried, and anxious about so many things that we can never confidently "sit."

It is one thing to trust the stability and support of a chair and quite another to trust others, God, and even ourselves. The way the Scouts completely trusted their chairs without thinking about it is a picture of childlike trust. As children, we engage others and the actions of our own bodies without thought or awareness. We show our emotions, wants, and needs wholeheartedly. We fall into the world—or at least our understanding of the world—without hesitation and completely rest on the love, care, and attention of those around us.

I remember the day when childlike trust was demonstrated for me by a three-year-old girl. She ran toward me with delight in her eyes, grabbed my hands, and threw herself back with abandon as her feet shot up in the air. I was aghast at how much she trusted me to hold on to her, and I was astounded at how much she trusted herself to hold on to me and complete her acrobatic move! She had little fear, if any. That's trust!

Belief versus Trust: Putting Our Hearts in Action

Childlike trust is different than belief. *Belief* is mental assent that something is so; *trust* is acting on that belief. The Scouts trusted their chairs because, in their experience, chairs were reliable. Trust in the stability of chairs has become second nature to us; we do not mentally confirm our belief in chairs before sitting down: We just sit!

There are some things we believe to be true, but we do not trust ourselves with or to them. Let me use the example of bungee jumping to make clear the distinction between belief and trust. "If I choose to jump off this bridge, I believe that the bungee cord attached to my ankles will prevent me from splashing into the river a hundred feet below." This is mental assent, a belief. Trust takes this one important and essential step further— the step off the bridge. As the comic strip character Snoopy would say, "Cowabunga!" Trust acts on a belief.

I use the extreme example of bungee jumping because, for many of us, our trust in others, God, and the world has been tested and perhaps broken. To trust again with a childlike assurance feels like jumping off a bridge. It's scary! It takes time to regain that trust. We may not yell "Cowabunga!" but we can learn to trust again with a certain amount of abandon that leads us to live life more fully.

When the Legs Give Out: Obstacles to Trust

The before-and-after difference of trusting and not trusting the chairs provides a snapshot of the difference between childlike trust and the diminishment or withholding of trust we learn as adults. In early childhood, we discern no boundaries between our self and the world around us. Trust comes easily because it has not been tested.

But as we grow up and develop self-awareness, we begin to play an increasingly active role in crafting the stories we tell, believe, and live by. These stories are a unique mix of trust and mistrust, beginning with our judgment, intuition, abilities, and talents, and these stories filter into and color our relationships. All of us, to varying degrees, have been hurt, disappointed, lied to, cheated on, abandoned, mistreated, abused, and cursed. We also have been loved, encouraged, confirmed, adored, celebrated, trusted, delighted in, helped, and blessed. As a result of these interactions, positive and negative, each one of us has a unique way of "sitting" in our relationships, and it is usually not comfortably, in the same way the Scouts demonstrated what it would be like to never quite completely trust the chair.

To compound matters, when our trust is repeatedly broken or abused, we develop a disposition of cynicism, a loss of hope, and an increase in anxiety. We come to view trust as synonymous with being naive, gullible, or—worse yet—ignorant. One of the best-known examples of trust-turned-gullible is Charlie Brown in the comic strip *Peanuts*. He believes that this time, finally, Lucy will not move the football when he tries to kick it—yet she does it every time. We admire Charlie Brown for his deep desire to kick a field goal and his unfailing trust in Lucy as his holder. But we also think he is gullible, stubborn, and dumb! Charlie Brown's trust in Lucy is blind trust—ultimately childish, not childlike.

Jesus's words, "Unless you change and become like children, you will never enter the kingdom of heaven," speak to this mixed bag of trust and mistrust, gullibility, suspicion, and cynicism. These words do not ask us to return to blind trust, but to a trust that has its eyes wide open, a trust that has gained wisdom and self-awareness. Childlike trust is vital to our ability to learn, have deep and meaningful relationships, try new things, better handle life's disappointments and failures, grow in our capacity for compassion for ourselves and others, willingly forgive, and share in deep relationships. To become like a child is to cultivate a disposition of trust, beginning with trust in ourselves.

Childlike Trust Begins with Resilience

How do children learn? Usually the hard way. Children trust and trust and trust until that trust is no longer sustainable. Unguarded in their hunger for experience, they naturally allow themselves to be vulnerable. (They're ignorant of the ways of the world, too, but more on that later.) They seem fine with the simple equation that learning and living have their requisite measure of falls, bumps, and painful experiences.

One Sunday morning before church, I watched a beautiful little girl named Sierra play in the sacristy. Sierra was at the age when her way of running meant she was perpetually off balance. It was as if she pushed her head forward and then expected her chubby little legs and feet to play catch-up. She was a study in being on the verge of a major fall-down-and-go-boom-boom. She fell on a regular basis—sometimes softly and sometimes with more authority—but, even after a big tumble and tears, she never failed to get back on her feet.

Sierra was the picture of resilience, which is what we as adults need to begin to regain childlike trust. We need to have the confidence that we will recover from our stumbles—and we will stumble. Alison Bonds Shapiro, remarkable survivor of two debilitating and nearly fatal strokes, includes a chapter called "Trusting Each Other: What Is Trust Anyway?" in her book *Healing into Possibility: The Transformational Lessons of a Stroke*. She points out that our failures contribute to our character development as much as our successes do. To try to avoid missteps to prevent feelings of hurt or disappointment hinders our ability to get to know our authentic selves.

> Being willing to know [who we are] is not the same as harshly judging. Harsh judgments close us off to ourselves. Compassion, forgiveness, and acceptance open us up and allow us to learn.
>
> If we know and accept our limitations without fighting that knowledge, we can learn to communicate what we know and don't know about what we can and cannot do. We come to understand that everybody has limitations. We see that we and our relationships are always transforming—never remaining static—giving us endless opportunities to keep on learning.[1]

Unlike Sierra, I ask that life be in perfect balance before I venture out, and I am not alone in this. Adults learn to play it safe, manipulating life so we expose ourselves to as little risk as possible. In the process, we stifle our own growth. In our attempts to avoid hurt and disappointment, we limit our capacity to experience life. We are hesitant to let others see our authentic selves—"the real me"—for fear of rejection, which prevents us from developing authentic relationships with others. Here again resilience comes in, together with our confidence in our own ability to recover. In *Daring to Trust: Opening Ourselves to Real Love and Intimacy*, noted therapist David Richo says, "The foundation of trust "is not 'you will never hurt me.' It is 'I trust myself with whatever you do.'"[2]

How have I played it safe? I have asked myself this question often and it never fails to reveal the subtle ways I settle for too much safety and too little life experience. I have avoided conflict, hidden my evolving theology, sat at home, stayed propped against the wall, kept quiet, remained in unfulfilling relationships and jobs, dreamed dreams without taking steps to fulfill them, and procrastinated when it comes to achieving my goals. But when I have trusted more in myself, my gifts, and talents; trusted more in others and the world; and trusted more in God's grace, I have faced conflict, lived my theology, gone out, danced, spoken my mind and heart, ended relationships and found new jobs, chased dreams, and worked hard to achieve my goals.

How are you playing it safe?

God Within: Restoring Our Sense of Safety

Sierra's ability to weather the stumbles and scrapes of learning to run is rooted, in part, in her sense that the world is safe. Her parents and grand-parents have helped cultivate this feeling of safety. When she tries some-thing new, skins her knee, and runs into the arms of her family members, they let her have a good cry and encourage her to try again: "It's going to be okay!" And in five minutes Sierra's back at it, with a bit more wisdom but with the same enthusiasm.

As adults, we know the world isn't always a safe place, and there aren't always people around us with open arms, ready to comfort and encourage us. So from what place do we conjure up our sense of safety, where we can return when we have skinned our hearts?

If we listen to Jesus's words, we find ourselves opening to safety and childlike trust in God. In the Sermon on the Mount in the Gospel of Matthew, Jesus encourages the crowd to trust God's loving, caring pres-ence when he says,

> Do not worry about your life, what you will eat or what you will drink, or about your body, what you will wear. Is not life more than food, and the body more than clothing? Look at the birds of the air; they neither sow nor reap nor gather into barns, and yet your heavenly Father feeds them. Are you not of more value than they? And can any of you by worrying add a single hour to your span of life? (Matthew 6:25–27)

Jesus invites us to trust the Love at the center of all things. This might seem naive, or even like pie-in-the-sky religion, but various other interpretations of this sentiment clarify this thinking as an inward focus on what's already within us. It isn't blind trust or a childish Pollyanna naiveté in which we act as though God has put a protective shield around us, allowing us to act thoughtlessly and with impunity. Rather, trusting God creates a place within our hearts for us to gather courage, find support, take comfort, and reconnect with our intuition. Spiritual teacher and best-selling author Marianne Williamson describes trust in God as a form of communication with the Sacred:

> I trust life not because I trust the world, but because I trust the God who lives in my heart. I try to remind myself not to go anywhere or do anything without asking for spiritual direction through prayer and meditation. I don't trust that there are no muggers in the park, no people who would mistreat my heart. But I trust my intuition, my common sense and my intelligence. I would not enter that park or that relationship or that business situation without first checking in with my internal radar, for that is how God speaks to us.[3]

Williamson's view of trusting God echoes Thomas Merton's classic prayer of trust:

> My Lord God, I have no idea where I am going. I do not see the road ahead of me. I cannot know for certain where it will end. Nor do I really know myself, and the fact that I think that I am following your will does not mean that I am actually doing so. But I believe that the desire to please you does in fact please you. And I hope I have that desire in all that I am doing. I hope that I will never do anything apart from that desire. And I know that if I do this you will lead me by the right road though I may know nothing about it. Therefore will I trust you always though I may seem to be lost and in the shadow of death. I will not fear, for you are ever with me, and you will never leave me to face my perils alone.[4]

Sister Joan Chittister, Benedictine nun and spiritual leader, similarly describes trust in God as a source of strength rather than an escape from the challenges of the real world. In fact, she describes her trust in God as the best spiritual advice she's ever received:

> I watched my mother weather every challenge, survive every loss, persist till every struggle turned to gain and trust every turn of her personal universe because her faith told her that there had to be meaning, purpose, and growth in every instant. "Just trust God,

Joan," she said over and over again, "and do not quit." That surrender to the God who, in the end, wishes us "well and not woe"
has been the mainstay of my life, both spiritual and personal.[5]

Resting Wholeheartedly in Trust

Poet David Whyte was sharing a glass of wine with monk David Steindl-
Rast when the poet David looked at the monk David and asked, "Tell me
about exhaustion." The monk David took a moment and then said, "You
know that the antidote to exhaustion is not necessarily rest." "What is it,
then?" asked the poet David. The monk David answered, "The antidote to
exhaustion is wholeheartedness."[6]

Much like we feel when we mistrust the stability of our chairs, lack of
trust leads to a life of worry, anxiety, and exhaustion. If we cannot "sit"
in ourselves, in relationships, in life, in God, as we usually sit in chairs,
we are unable to rest. To give ourselves to something, to someone, to life
wholeheartedly is to do it with childlike trust. This involves trusting our
own ability to discern in whom to place our trust, and to extricate ourselves from those relationships and situations where that trust is not val-
ued, knowing that we will recover from the pain of doing so.

Practices

A Heart Checkup

Set aside at least 30 minutes and respond honestly to the following
questions.

Where am I, or with whom am I, halfhearted?

Where am I, or with whom am I, coldhearted?

Where am I, or with whom am I, hardhearted?

What am I, or who am I, wholehearted about?

Where would I, or with whom would I, like to be more wholehearted?

An Exercise in Trust

Find a very comfortable chair or couch and settle in. Take a few minutes to breathe deeply and just relax. Now notice how deeply and completely you trust the chair or couch you are resting on.

What does that feel like?

What or whom in your life do you trust to that same degree?

2 Humble Me

FINDING YOUR TRUE SELF IN AUTHENTIC HUMILITY

> When "true self" is the topic, children are the best
> source, because they live so close to their birthright gifts.
>
> PARKER J. PALMER

When the hostess at a Palm Springs restaurant said to the family, "Follow me, please, I'll take you to your table," Dezi, dressed in a princess outfit and fancy shoes, her head of curls tilted back regally, took a big stride forward and struck a pose for the hostess. The hostess said, "Oh, my, you look so beautiful!"

Dezi, the lovely princess, led the family procession as they followed the hostess to a table at the far end of a mostly empty restaurant. When they finished their dinner, the restaurant was full of people and, on the way out, Dezi looked side to side as she batted her eyes and sashayed back and forth, stopping at each table, waving to her royal subjects who couldn't help but *ooh* and *aah* at the beautiful princess in their midst. When Dezi reached the lobby, she announced, "I have the biggest wedgie!" and daintily readjusted her tights!

Humble Like a Child?

What comes to mind when you think of becoming humble? Put others first, think of yourself last. The needs of others take precedence over your own. Aim to be modest. Avoid being arrogant or assertive.

11

These are all aspects of being humble, but is that an accurate description of a child? I don't think so.

Just after Jesus says we must become like children to enter the kingdom of heaven, he goes on to say, "Whoever becomes humble like this child is the greatest in the kingdom of heaven" (Matthew 18:4). Humble like a child? What was Jesus thinking?

Children tend to think of themselves first, their needs come first, they always want to be first. They are assertive and want to get their way. They would rather throw a tantrum in a crowded supermarket than defer or submit to an adult's wishes. *Modest* is not a word that describes their sense of importance. *Grandiose* would be far better.

But we go too far if we say that children are egotists. Children—who haven't yet developed a self-image—don't have the ability to reflect on themselves or to consciously analyze how others see them. They each have an incredibly active imagination and try on all kinds of personas, but they have not yet learned the subtle adult art form of self-deception. They cannot help but be who they are. Here lies the root of genuine humility as seen in a child.

Living Close to the Truth

Children are naturally true to themselves. If they are mad, they show it. If they are hungry, they tell you. If they get hurt, they cry and run to a caring adult for comfort. If they want something, they go after it. If they are scared, they cry out. If they are happy, they laugh. If they feel love, they express it unabashedly. They tell you what they think without filter. Children live and express the truth of their experience. Our love of children, our fascination with children, is rooted in this very lack of pretense or premeditation. What you see is what you get!

But as we grow up, we learn to be who our family, teachers, friends, and society want us to be. Unconsciously at first, and then with more intention, we craft who we think we need to be in order to be accepted, loved, rewarded, admired, and successful. We hide and bury the unacceptable parts, and put what we think is our best foot forward, constantly measuring ourselves against the people and images around us in order to make it in the world.

Such artifice, besides being exhausting, makes genuine, childlike humility difficult to cultivate because we are trying to be true to things outside us, instead of being true to ourselves. We are not real. In his book *A Guide to Living in the Truth: Saint Benedict's Teaching on Humility*, Cistercian monk Michael Casey defines humility simply as truth and a willingness to act on it. The Latin root for the word *humble* is *humus*, which means "ground." It suggests being of the earth, down to earth, grounded in reality. Humility is achieved by living close to, and by being grounded in, the truth of our being. This truth involves acknowledging all that we are—our strengths and our weaknesses, the areas in which we can grow and our personal limitations.

Andre Agassi, the long-tressed, image-is-everything tennis prodigy, rocketed to the top of the tennis world, but after his 1997 loss to Pat Rafter in the semifinals at Wimbledon, he plummeted to the rank of 141st in professional tennis. He kept losing in early rounds to far less talented players. His coach Brad Gilbert told Agassi he was a shadow of his formal self, as a person and as a tennis star, and he suggested Agassi return to the tennis world's equivalent of the minor leagues to get back into form. Agassi, to the surprise of many, did just that, and he returned a different person. I remember reading an article in the *San Francisco Chronicle* where Agassi said of his coach, "He was brutally honest. The truth is a good thing if you allow it to work for you." Andre Agassi heard a difficult truth about himself, was humbled by it, and he allowed it to work for him, helping him live closer to the truth of who he was. It had a direct effect on his performance on the court and in his life.

Letting the Truth Work for You ... and Humble You

The self-image we develop and maintain in adulthood is a combination, in varying degrees, of overvaluation and undervaluation. It is part wishful thinking, part outdated upbringing, part cultural myth, and part reality. Knowing on some level that we are not true to ourselves, nor knowing what our true self entails, we tend to compensate either by puffing ourselves up with pride or devaluing ourselves with shame.

Healthy pride involves taking genuine satisfaction in and enjoying our real talent, accomplishments, and personality. Healthy shame is a genuine response to our own failure to live according to our deepest values and live into who we really are. Both emotions are important for us to recognize and experience. But pride as overcompensation and shame as undercompensation are detrimental to living close to the truth. To become humble like a child means pulling our self-image in line with reality and letting truth work for us. And that is the tricky part.

Pride as Overcompensation

St. Augustine defines pride as "the love of one's own excellence." In this sense, pride is a mask. It hides our insecurity, anxiety, and fear of not being good enough. We make a mistake when we criticize others for what we see as being too full of themselves—for in reality they are empty; they are trying to be who they are not. Beloved Quaker author Parker J. Palmer writes,

> I have met too many people who suffer from an empty self. They have a bottomless pit where their identity should be—an inner void they try to fill with competitive success, consumerism, sexism, racism, or anything that might give them the illusion of being better than others. We embrace attitudes and practices such as these not because we regard ourselves as superior but because we have no sense of self at all. Putting others down becomes a path to identity, a path we would not need to walk if we knew who we were.[1]

There is no doubt that pride taxes our energy and, inevitably, damage follows in its wake, but a previous damage is the cause of pride. Proverbs 16:18 says, "Pride goes before destruction, a haughty spirit before a fall." But not being true to ourselves goes before pride; an empty self goes before a puffing up.

A story in the Gospel of Luke contrasts a person who is proud, a Pharisee, with one who is humble, a tax collector.

> Two men went up to the temple to pray, one a Pharisee and the other a tax collector. The Pharisee, standing by himself, was praying thus, "God, I thank you that I am not like other people: thieves, rogues, adulterers, or even like this tax collector. I fast twice a week; I give a tenth of all my income." But the tax collector, standing far off, would not even look up to heaven, but was beating his

breast and saying, "God, be merciful to me, a sinner!" I tell you, this man went down to his home justified rather than the other; for all who exalt themselves will be humbled, but all who humble themselves will be exalted. (Luke 18:10–14)

We must be careful here. The Pharisee's problem is not in giving thanks for his abilities or position, but in using them to justify his attitude of feeling superior to another. If he were humble, the Pharisee might have prayed this way:

Thank you, God, for all the powers of heart and mind that enable me to fast twice a week and give tithes of all that I have. Truly, my lot in life has fallen in an abundant place. I cannot begin to know all the pressures on the tax collector next to me, tempting him to work for an occupying enemy. I do not know the mystery of his heart. Let your compassion surround him. Bring him back to your pathway of peace, and reveal to me the ways I fall short and my secret faults.

Shame as Undercompensation

The other response to not being true to ourselves is to deflate the ego. Instead of displaying an unwarranted pride in our accomplishments, we devalue and minimize our gifts and talents. We are ashamed of ourselves, full of self-recrimination, and feel we are unlovable. Here the emptiness is exposed and taken to the extreme, becoming an excuse for our lot in life. Just as we bristle in the presence of those who puff themselves up, we become exasperated by those who constantly belittle and shame themselves.

Ten years ago I had a memorable run-in with my own prideful overcompensation and shameful undercompensation. At a family reunion I met my younger cousins Allen (age ten) and Christiana (age eight) for the first time. We went swimming in the hotel pool. I had known them for all of half an hour, when Allen said, "You don't have very much hair!"

My reaction was a study in the temptation not to let the truth work for me. My first thought was, *I have more hair than you think! At least I'm not as hairless as my bald friend Harry!* In a split second I puffed myself up—in spite of reality—and compared myself favorably to my friend Harry. The next second, I reversed direction and became shame-filled. *Yes, I am losing my hair, faster and faster all the time. Everyone in this pool is probably thinking, "Poor guy, he's really going bald."* Both of my reactions were examples of refusing to let the truth work for me. Once I recognized both of my reactions, and took a few deep breaths, I found myself saying to this ten-year-old harbinger of reality, "You know, you're right." And I was surprised at how good it felt to live closer to the truth.

It is not easy to let go of pride, to release our sense of self-importance and our tendency to judge ourselves in comparison with others. It benefits us to remember Jesus's words when he washed the feet of his disciples at the last supper:

> You call me Teacher and Lord—and you are right, for that is what I am. So if I, your Lord and Teacher, have washed your feet, you also ought to wash one another's feet. For I have set you an example, that you also should do as I have done to you. Very truly, I tell you, servants are not greater than their master, nor are messengers greater than the one who sent them. If you know these things, you are blessed if you do them. (John 13:13–17)

It is also not easy to let go of undervaluing or shaming ourselves. It helps to remember that we are beloved sons and daughters of God, created in God's image, with unique gifts, talents, personalities, and souls. There is no one just like us. As Jesus reminded us, we are the light of the world. And in the Gospel of John, Jesus says, "I do not call you servants any longer ... but I have called you friends" (15:15).

How do we walk the fine line between the overcompensation of pride and the undercompensation of shame? We can start by seeking the truth about ourselves. We tend to define something in only one way. But the truth, more often than not, is paradoxical in nature. The paradoxical truth about ourselves is that as human beings we have weaknesses and strengths, limitations and potential for growth. This duality is reflected in the following two writings. The first, from the Apostle Paul's letter to the Romans, shows our human weakness and frailty:

> I do not understand my own actions. For I do not do what I want, but I do the very thing I hate.... I can will what is right, but I

cannot do it. For I do not do the good I want, but the evil I do not want is what I do. (7:15, 18–19)

The second, from Marianne Williamson, shows our human giftedness and potential:

Our deepest fear is not that we are inadequate. Our deepest fear is that we are powerful beyond measure. It is our light, not our darkness, that most frightens us. We ask ourselves, who am I to be brilliant, gorgeous, talented, and fabulous? Actually, who are you not to be? You are a child of God. Your playing small doesn't serve the world. There's nothing enlightened about shrinking so that other people won't feel insecure around you. We were born to make manifest the glory of God that is within us. It's not just in some of us, it's in everyone.[2]

Childlike humility involves putting away our insecurities and understanding that both our weaknesses and our strengths are blessings. Identifying our strengths means we can use them to help others. Knowing our weaknesses will help us temper our own self-importance and show more compassion to others when their weaknesses are revealed.

A Long, Loving Look at the Real

It takes courage and patience to seek the truth about ourselves in our practice of humility. In spiritual direction there is a phrase we use to describe this work, first coined by Jesuit theologian Walter Burghardt. We encourage others "to take a long, loving look at the real."[3] This look at the real is, first of all, a *long* look. We often cannot see the truth in the first glance or two—or twenty—yet first impressions about others and situations are often as far as we go. It takes time to see past our carefully constructed or unconsciously assumed self-images and God-images. It takes time to see the patterns and habits formed over the course of our lives. It takes time to let go of what is false and embrace what is real and true.

After a strenuous hike in Yosemite National Park, my girlfriend, Julie, and I decided to take it easy the following day and go on a leisurely hike to Mirror Lake from Curry Village. After about a mile of gentle walking, we reclined on the grass in a large meadow for lunch. We laid back and gazed at the stunning scenery around us. The strenuous hike the previous day had offered amazing views, and we had often stopped to wonder at the beauty and to take pictures, but lying in the meadow had a completely different feel to it. We were not in a rush, and the long look made the beauty around us come alive.

The long look allows what is there to unfold, and we are often surprised at just how much more there is to be seen and experienced.

Second, this look at the real is a *loving* look. No harsh self-judgments here—only compassion for who we are, no matter what we discover about ourselves. This loving look at ourselves is patterned after the loving look of God, who knows everything about us and loves us beyond measure. Nothing can separate us from God, not even the truth about us. In fact, living close to the truth means living closer to God.

Third, this look is not so much a matter of seeing as it is a matter of receiving. It is not an aggressive, analytical look, but a contemplative opening of our hearts and minds to see and experience the truth that is there. The word *contemplate*—literally, "with temple"—captures much of the meaning of this attitude of waiting for the deepest truths to be revealed.

Finally, within the quest to become humble like a child is the invitation to see and embrace the real, leaving behind what is false. This refers not only to falsehoods or lies, but also to what Thomas Merton called the false self. We leave behind the self-image built up to please others, curry the favor of our culture, and make us compare favorably to others. Franciscan priest and spiritual writer Richard Rohr writes in *Immortal Diamond: The Search for Our True Self*,

> Your False Self is quite good and necessary as far as it goes. It just does not go far enough, and it often poses and thus substitutes for the real thing. That is its only problem, and that is why we call it "false." The False Self is bogus more than bad, and bogus only when it pretends to be more than it is. Various false selves (temporary costumes) are necessary to get us all started, and they show their limitations when they stay around too long. If a person keeps growing, his or her various false selves usually die in exposure to greater light.[4]

Again, abandoning your false self is no easy task. Best-selling author Sue Monk Kidd, in her book *When the Heart Waits*, offers a prayer that captures well the difficulties of this work:

> God, I don't want to live falsely, in self-imposed prisons and fixed, comfortable patterns that confine my soul and diminish the truth in me. So much of me has gone underground. I want to let my soul out. I want to be free to risk what's true, to be myself. Set free the daring in me—the willingness to go within, to see the self-lies. I'll try to run away, but don't let me. Don't let me stifle myself with prudence that binds the creative re-visioning of life and the journey toward wholeness. I'm scared, God. Make me brave. Lead me into the enormous spaces of becoming. Help me cease the small, tedious work of maintaining and protecting so that I can break the masks that obscure your face shining in the night of my own soul. Help me to green my soul and risk becoming the person you created me to be. Tomorrow I may regret these words, but tonight I speak them, for I know that you're somewhere inside them, that you love me and won't leave me alone in their echo.[5]

Climbing the Ladder of Truth to Childlike Humility

Bernard of Clairvaux, a twelfth-century abbot, suggested a threefold process of humility that involves climbing the ladder of truth. The first rung on the ladder is to know yourself. Humility begins when we embrace the whole truth of who we are. As spiritual director Robert Corin Morris writes, "While boasting may be the opposite of humility, true humility is not the result of self-deprecation. It is, rather, the fruit of a keen-eyed ability to see oneself realistically, as a flawed and gifted creature like all other human beings."[6]

This knowing of self is not a speculative or an intellectual knowledge, but an experiential knowledge and acceptance of all that we are. And who are we? This may be the trickiest part of all. We are complex and nuanced. We are beloved creations of God, made in God's image, endowed with gifts and talents as well as human limitations and frailties.

The second rung of the ladder of truth is to know our neighbors, our fellow human beings, and to treat them with compassion. They are the same as we are: glorious, fallible creatures, embraced by God's love. *Compassion* means to "feel with," not only in suffering and sorrow, but also in celebration and joy. Knowing our neighbors also means being with them in solidarity, forging a common bond with all others that results in a profound reverence for every person and seeks justice for all. The idea of the kingdom of heaven is built on this sensibility that we are one.

The third rung of the ladder of truth is to know God in an intimate way. I believe it was Bernard of Clairvaux who wrote, "Yes, we come to know in some frightening, almost terrifying way, that we are, all of us, one in and with the living God, the Godhead who embraces us with the fierce intimacy of an intensely passionate lover." Truth enables us to know God as love, and to know that we are loved and accepted by God, just as we are.

Finding the True Face of Humility

If it is as Jesus said, that we must cultivate childlike humility in order to fully embrace God's grace, then we must live closer to the truth of our souls. The challenge is that, as Rainer Maria Rilke says in *The Book of Hours*, "We come of age as masks. Our true face never speaks."[7] Childlike humility, then, means removing the masks we have learned to wear, acquainting ourselves with our true voice, and letting our true self speak.

Practices

I Am ...

Complete the following sentence until you run out of answers:

"I am ..."

After you feel as if you've exhausted your responses, stay with it and come up with ten more responses:

"I am ..."

Whatever you append to the phrase "I am ..." is a profound window into your self-image, sense of identity, the roles you play, what you feel, and what you believe to be true about yourself. Once you've come up with your responses, take each response and say it aloud several times. Then ask yourself these questions:

✓ Where and/or who did this come from?

What category does this fall into? Is it a feeling? Is it a role I play in society or my family systems? Is it my vocation, job, or calling? Is it an attitude, a way of being, a character trait, or a flaw?

What surprises you about your answers?

Now that you've examined your responses more fully, revisit each one and think about its accuracy. Completing the phrase "I am ..." often tends to produce a global statement that suggests it is true of you all the time, such as "I am always such a pessimist" or "I am never good at finishing anything."

Recast each such response, replacing the *I am* statement with more nuanced language, carefully choosing verbs, adverbs, adjectives, and qualifiers to craft a more truthful statement. Refining the two examples above might sound like this: "I find that when I'm not feeling confident or when I'm not thinking very clearly, I tend to be more pessimistic. But when I feel safe and sure, I am more optimistic." "I remember my dad would say to me that I never finished anything, but when I look at my life objectively I have finished many projects and goals and have done them quite well."

Observe how your sense of self and your feelings change as you rewrite your responses in a way that is closer to the truth.

Who Are You?

Another way to do this practice is to pair up in groups of two or three and take turns asking each other to respond to this question:

"Who are you?"

The first ten or fifteen responses might evoke things such as "a businessman," "a Christian," "an optimist," "a mother of two teenagers," "a wife and grandmother." But keep asking:

"Who are you?"

As you do, you will find the answers moving into other categories, such as feelings ("angry," "confused," "grateful"), sense of place in life ("adrift," "lost," "finally able to be myself"), and ways of being or a deep sense of self ("creative," "an adventurer," "a beloved child of God," "a shipwreck").

As the person asking "Who are you?" write down the responses of each other person so they have a written record to refer back to. Once everyone in the dyad or triad has had a turn to respond, take the time silently to rewrite your own responses with greater nuance, and then take turns sharing with each other several of the rewritten responses that seem important for you to highlight.

A Long, Loving Look at the Real

If you are facing an ongoing discernment issue or struggling with an important decision, take a (1) long, (2) loving, (3) look at the (4) real.

Long: Take 20 minutes now, or, if you'd like to go deeper, 15 minutes each day for the next seven days, to look at the situation or decision from as many perspectives as you can. Don't so much analyze it as let it show you what's there. Just slowing the pace down can remove much of the anxiety from the situation.

Loving: Look at the issue you are facing with as much love as possible. Consider all the people involved and all that influences and affects them.

Look: There are many different ways to look at something: an aggressive, prying glare; a cold, analytical scan; an apathetic, disinterested glance; a suspicious, skeptical stare; a judgmental, critical projection of your own fears, frustrations, or anger. Your situation might call for different kinds of looks. There is a place for the contemplative, receptive, open-eyed look; the objective, searching analysis; and more. What does each kind of look reveal to you?

Real: Finally, what is the real in your situation? Have previous ways of looking at the situation blinded you to aspects of what's real?

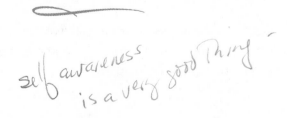

3 A Burning Bush in Every Backyard

RESTORING YOUR CAPACITY FOR AWE AND WONDER

I am mentally preparing myself for
the five-year-old mind.
I want to come down to their physical limitations
and up to their sense of wonder and awe.

SHINICHI SUZUKI

Look at everything always as though you were
seeing it either for the first or last time: Thus
is your time on earth filled with glory.

BETTY SMITH

One Saturday Bruce, a pastor friend of mine, went to watch his young nephew, David, play soccer. David's coach wasn't too demanding; the kids could learn to play soccer and enjoy it, too. The other team's coach opted for the approach of Al Davis of Oakland Raiders fame—"Just win, baby!"—and yanked kids from the game if they weren't doing it right. David's team was getting pummeled. The parents, thinking the support-ers of the other team were becoming a bit too smug for their own good, began to encourage David and his teammates to play a little harder. My friend was soon yelling alongside the other parents for David's team to beat the you-know-what out of their opponents. Forget having fun, beat 'em like a drum! Just when it looked like David's team was about to score, David dropped to his knees in the middle of the field and began yelling. David's teammates ran over and knelt down next to him. Was David hurt? No. It seems that David had found a very cool caterpillar. The other team, meanwhile, found it easy to score with an empty net on the other end of the field. Even the goalie from David's team had left his post to wonder at this caterpillar that survived in the face of bouncing balls and cleated feet.

A Capacity for Awe and Wonder

Children have an incredible capacity for and receptivity to wonder, awe, and mystery. And they don't just marvel at the big things—rainbows, sunsets, tornados. They notice caterpillars, sparkly things on the ground, and spiderwebs shimmering in the light. They are open to holy distraction. Only for adults has the world become mundane. We've gotten used to it, we've seen it before, we know the answers. We're unimpressed with things that don't grab or demand our attention, or we're too rushed to care.

More often than not, we lose our sense of mystery without even knowing it. After the soccer game, my friend confessed that he had gotten too caught up in the competition. He felt embarrassed that his nephew's team wasn't playing well and disappointed that David was so easily distracted from what was important. But then Bruce had an epiphany: The problem wasn't his nephew's; it was his own. He had let pride, a competitive spirit, the rules of the game, and the expectations of others define what was important. These things prevented him from noticing caterpillars. He was stunned to realize he made very little room in his life for wonder and awe.

In his book *Orthodoxy*, Catholic theologian G. K. Chesterton notes that we need to find a balance between usual patterns of behavior—what we know—and the mystery in all that surrounds us.

> How can we contrive to be at once astonished at the world and yet at home in it? … How can this world give us at once the fascination of a strange town and the comfort and honor of being our own town? … We need so to view the world as to combine an idea

of wonder and an idea of welcome. We need to be happy in this wonderland without once being merely comfortable.[1]

What we miss when we don't try to see past the dullness of our own complacency! One of the most powerful stories of wonder and awe can be found in Exodus 3: Moses and the burning bush. Moses was tending his father-in-law's flocks when something caught his eye. Rather than ignoring the impulse to get on with his work, Moses turned his attention to this burning bush. Only when God saw that Moses was receptive did God reveal himself to Moses. Moses's receptivity, his capacity for wonder and awe, opened him up for an encounter with the Divine, and he found himself on holy ground.

All of Life a Sacrament

Well, who wouldn't turn aside and pay attention to a burning bush that was not consumed by the fire? But that assumes the bush was literally on fire. There is another way to understand how it might have burned.

Several years ago I went hiking in a state park near Santa Cruz, California, and I was, I'll admit, a bit lost, when I accidentally wandered into the middle of a grove of sequoias. At first I saw them, and then I really *saw* them. The first seeing was with the eyes of sight: a grove of sequoias. The second seeing was with the eyes of wonder and awe. Their majestic red trunks rose around me like pillars, reaching up into the hazy afternoon light, their branches creating a dappled canopy, a quiet, holy place. I *had* to stop. The grove enveloped me like a cathedral, and the stillness roared in my senses. The forest was on fire with the presence of the Sacred. It burned bright with the light of life. Just as Moses learned from the burning bush that God's name was "I Am," I too knew beyond a shadow of a doubt that, embraced by this grove of burning sequoias, the presence of Love was at the heart of all things.

Such experiences are not reserved only for state and national parks. We only need to become like a child and burning bushes might appear anywhere and at any time. Twentieth-century Jewish philosopher Abraham Joshua Heschel describes this childlike awe as the ability "to sense in small things the beginning of infinite significance, to sense the ultimate in the common and simple."[2] Life itself can be a sacrament if we but see it.

In *A Field Guide to the Soul*, spiritual teacher James Thornton warns us of the life-changing effects of opening ourselves up to this kind of wonder and awe:

> Be careful. If you let yourself feel this wonder, you will be lost. You will never get over it. It will become the center of your life. The consequences will be dramatic, and you risk being labeled an eccentric by your fellow humans: life will begin to make sense; meaning will come into your life unbidden; doubt will drop away and you will know who you are.[3]

An ancient story tells of three princes from the island of Ceylon who set out in pursuit of great treasure. They never found the treasure for which they searched, but along the way they were continually surprised by treasures they never anticipated. The original name of Ceylon was Serendip, and thus the ancient story is titled "The Three Princes of Serendip." From that story an eighteenth-century British man of letters, Horace Walpole, coined the word *serendipity*. Serendipity occurs when we are receptive and open to finding wonder in the monotonous and the mundane.

The Costs of Our Fear of Change

Becoming like a child, reconnecting with our inner sense of wonder and awe, involves change: a change of heart, a change of perspective, a change in a way of being. It is a conversion of sorts. For adults, this change, this conversion, can be discomforting. Poet and spiritual writer Kathleen Norris muses,

> Conversion is frightening to oneself, and to others, precisely because it can seem like a regression. One's adult certainty about the nature of the world is shaken, and this can feel like being sent back to square one.[4]

This discomfort can be seen in the response of Nicodemus to Jesus when Jesus tells him in the Gospel of John, "You must be born again" (3:3). Nicodemus asks how one can go back to the womb. You can almost hear him saying, "How dare you tell me, an adult, a learned one at that, to go back to square one!"

Going back to the beginning means letting go of what we think we know to be true and the comfort of familiarity. It also requires a willingness to step into the unknown. These actions are not easily embraced. An article published ten years ago in the *Contra Costa Times* spotlighted how technology was redefining "roughing it" in the wilderness. The article did not need to be read; the accompanying photograph said it all. There sat two teenage boys in lawn chairs. Behind them, surrounding them, stood the forest, the mystery of wilderness. In front of them sat a large television, wires trailing from the back, and in their hands were game-boy control panels. In the middle of nature, the teenagers were playing video games, their eyes narrowly focused on the TV, their brows furrowed in competition, their minds occupied and distracted, their souls oblivious to the surrounding wonder, awe, and mystery.

Many of us adults can place ourselves in those lawn chairs. Having become so used to being entertained and distracted, we may have forgotten the real taste of wonder and awe. Thus we're unwilling to give up what we know and superficially enjoy. Yet we cannot encounter mystery—refamiliarize ourselves with the thrilling juiciness of wonder—with game-boy control panels, or manage it with a remote control. To be receptive to wonder and awe is to be receptive to God. Theologian Karl Rahner writes, "God is the Mystery we call God."[5]

Or it may be out of fear that we settle for distraction, for entertainment, for anything but an encounter with wonder and awe. A friend of theologian Gerald May articulated this fear in a moment of candor:

> I never do anything which will make me feel too good, because when I feel very, very good I start to marvel at the wonder of being alive. And then I become frightened. Partly it's because the more I feel the beauty of being here on this earth the more I realize how fragile life is; how easily it can stop. And partly it's because I just don't know what to do with it all. I know I can spoil it if I try to touch it, or even if I think about it. But it's almost intolerable just to let it be. No, I'm really much more comfortable when I'm not too close to the wonder of life. When I've got problems or distractions or something to struggle with I feel much better, because then at least I know who I am and what I need to do.[6]

Mystery Is Not Solved, But Plumbed

In order to encounter mystery, May says, we must be willing to risk some degree of fear, but also be willing to surrender our habitual tendencies to either solve or ignore mystery. These two conditions together, according to May, make up the essence of contemplative spirituality. This contemplation is, in essence, a childlike experience:

> [True contemplation is] a totally uncluttered appreciation of existence, a state of mind or a condition of the soul that is simultaneously wide-awake and free from all preoccupation, precondition, and interpretation. It is a wonder-filled yet utterly simple experience.[7]

From this perspective we might rethink the well-known verse in Proverbs 9:10: "The fear of the Lord is the beginning of wisdom." A healthy fear—a reverence—means we are still changeable, malleable, teachable.

Wonder as Prayer

The receptivity of a child, the capacity for unencumbered wonder and awe, is a form of prayer, a direct link to gratitude. This thanksgiving is recognition for both gift and Giver. "Prayer does not 'want,'" says Kathleen Norris. "It is ordinary experience lived with gratitude and wonder."[8]

Bruce's nephew David, busy playing soccer, was drawn to an undulating caterpillar. The three princes of Serendip, busy looking for treasure, found treasures more priceless. Moses, busy tending his father-in-law's flocks, was drawn to a burning bush that was not consumed and, as a result, experienced the great "I Am."

If we allow the dip of the serene into our everyday lives, open up to wonder, allow ourselves to be captured by awe, and become receptive; if we face our fears of change and become like children, there will be a burning bush in every backyard. Because the great "I Am" is everywhere and in all things, we just need to take the time to open our eyes and really see. As the poet Walt Whitman observes,

> When I heard the learn'd astronomer,
> When the proofs, the figures, were ranged in columns before me;

When I was shown the charts and diagrams, to add, divide, measure
    them,
When I sitting heard the astronomer where he lectured with much
    applause in the lecture room,
How soon unaccountable I became tired and sick,
Till rising and gliding out I wander'd off by myself,
In the mystical moist night-air, and from time to time,
Look'd up in perfect silence at the stars.

Practices

Simply Notice

Set aside 15 to 30 minutes to do nothing but notice and take in all that is around you. You have no agenda here, nothing to accomplish—which goes against the cultural pressure to always be doing something productive. Resist the inclination to judge, analyze, figure out, make up stories, interpret, or categorize what you see, hear, and experience.

What happens when we cease our normal way of "seeing" things? Become aware of what you notice and how you feel. Try to take this sense of awareness with you into the rest of your day.

Specifically Notice

Choose an object—a plant, a vase, a painting ... anything, really—and spend 15 to 30 minutes writing down everything you can about that one object. (Don't worry about writing in full sentences.) In the first few minutes you will notice the more obvious things (color, size, pattern, smell, texture, uses), but then you will begin to notice connections and subtle things, such as who made it and the materials that went into it.

Notice how you feel now about the object after you have spent time really seeing it. What particularly lovely or inspiring thing about this object can you take with you into the coming days as a touchstone of wonder?

Things in Themselves

Set aside 15 to 30 minutes, in any kind of setting. Observe the people and things around you, and try to see them as having no utility to you whatsoever. For example, the tree is not meant to give you shade, or provide wood for your house, or its fruit for you to eat. The tree has a life of its own, separate from any use to you. How does seeing the tree this way help you see the tree itself?

This is a way of seeing things or people in and of themselves, without their being in any way beneficial to you.

What happens when you see this way?

How do you feel toward the things and people around you?

How do you feel toward yourself?

Walking Meditation

Take a walk in nature simply to be in nature. Pay attention to what you see, hear, and feel. Notice the effect nature has on your mood, attitude, thoughts, and feelings.

How does being in nature affect the balance of your levels of anxiety and trust, complaint and gratitude, emptiness and fulfillment, openheartedness and closed-heartedness?

What is one situation or area of your life that you particularly need balance in? Focus on that situation and see if you can let the wonder and awe of being in nature bring you a sense of balance.

4 The Eyes of Innocence

SEEING AS GOD SEES

Here [spiritual] formation flows from the belief
that we are born with souls in perfect form.
As time goes on, we are subject to powers of
deformation, from within as without, that twist
us into shapes alien to the shape of the soul. But
the soul never loses its original form and never
stops calling us back to our birthright integrity.

PARKER J. PALMER

In its highest form, not judging is the
ultimate act of forgiveness.

JOHN KUYPERS

In the middle of a lecture, Dr. James E. Loder, then a professor of Christian education at Princeton Theological Seminary, recounted his encounter with an elderly woman at a small grocery store on Nassau Street in Princeton, New Jersey. The encounter began when she almost ran into him with her shopping cart as she bullied her way around the store, a scowl etched on her face. Impatient, she cut people off and berated the staff for not being able to find what she wanted. Dr. Loder avoided her as much as he could as he shopped for groceries, but at the checkout counter he found himself face to face with her when she cut in front of him in line. He thought about saying something, but chickened out.

31

To Dr. Loder's surprise, the woman's demeanor suddenly changed drastically. A little boy, seated backward in the shopping cart in front of her, began to coo and devote total attention to the wrinkled face in front of him. The elderly woman softened, became kind, affectionate, and friendly. She chatted amiably with the child's mother. The child waved bye-bye to the elderly woman, who returned the wave and farewell remarks in her own childlike voice until the boy left the store. But it wasn't long before Dr. Loder witnessed the return of Mrs. Jekyll, cursing under her breath to the clerk about the price of food.

The Power of a Look of Innocence

Does our way of seeing affect others? If so, how? And how does it affect how we live our lives and relate to others? After recounting the story of the elderly woman, Dr. Loder asked the class to consider her demeanor and why it changed. Did the elderly woman perhaps think that other people saw her as an old lady, while the child looked at her with innocent eyes, seeing her for who she really was beneath the age, the wrinkles, the protective wall she'd erected over many years of life?

Having innocent eyes is a way of seeing the world unburdened by the cumulative pejorative connotations we gather as we mature. For example, a child isn't born fearing or hating people from other faith traditions. This kind of reaction is learned from others, usually adults. The same is true when it comes to our reactions to people of different classes or races. Marguerite Wright, in *I'm Chocolate, You're Vanilla: Raising Healthy Black and Biracial Children in a Race-Conscious World*, writes, "Kids don't think like us. They don't know race the way we know race."[1] She quotes a typical conversation with a child:

> "What color are you?"
> "You know what color. I'm red."
> "You're red?"
> "No, blue."

Children see color and difference, but it makes no difference to them. Difference has no negative connotation; it is welcomed with freshness and curiosity. We can learn from the way children see.

Having innocent eyes involves seeing past the exterior and into the essence of another person, as God sees humanity. The prophet Samuel learned this lesson. According to 1 Samuel 16:1–7, Samuel was appointed by God to anoint the next king of Israel. He looked first at the eldest son of Jesse, Eliab, who was tall and good-looking. "Surely this is the one!" he said to himself. Not so fast, God warned. Humans look on the outside and make judgments about the inside, but God looks into the heart. When Samuel looked past the outside features and into the hearts of Eliab and his brothers, he saw it was only David, the youngest, who had the righteous heart to be king.

A member of my former congregation in California, a delightful young woman with mental challenges, displayed this kind of insight while responding to a congregational survey as they searched for a new pastor:

> It doesn't matter to me whether our pastor is a man or a woman, just as long as they are a good pastor. I basically don't care and am not prejudiced. Also, I feel strongly in my heart that GOD isn't prejudiced either. He likes all people whether they are black, white, red, purple, etc. GOD likes everybody the same I think, even if they are bad people.

Losing the Eyes of Innocence

We all begin life with the eyes of innocence, but inevitably and necessarily our eyes become clouded with judgment as we grow older. The powerful influences of parenting, education, and culture, and experiences of love, fear, failure, success, and broken trust lead to biased ways of seeing. We become captive to our own judgments. For example, my father—a wonderful man and an accomplished teacher and counselor—had a disdain for men who were loud. I have faint memories of stories he would tell me as a child of uncles, brothers in arms, and fellow church members who were "too loud," an indicator of an outsized ego and untrustworthiness. As I grew up, his judgments became my own, not only about other men but also about myself. I could not allow myself to exhibit any behaviors or attitudes that fell into the category of "too loud." It has taken me years to undo the effect of that way of seeing and thinking, and to this day I still have a visceral reaction to anyone who is "too loud."

We cannot rid ourselves of making judgments—each day is chock-full of decisions that have an impact on ourselves, our families, and the world. But we can become more deeply aware of our judgments and the values, beliefs, experiences, and assumptions behind them. With this awareness, we can free ourselves of the judgmental thinking that holds us captive to our history, and liberate ourselves for new experiences, personal growth, and authentic relationships with others. Reclaiming the eyes of innocence unlocks the door imprisoning us, providing the necessary freedom through which change and transformation begin.

In the story of Jesus and Zacchaeus, in the Gospel of Luke, we see an example of this gift of innocence and its power to free someone from ingrained ways of being. In chapter 18, the author of the Gospel of Luke tells two stories. The first story, which we examined in chapter 2, is of a Pharisee and a tax collector. In first-century Palestine, under Roman imperial rule, the tax collector was a traitor and a thief. He worked for the occupying forces of Rome and often overtaxed his own people in order to feather his own nest. A tax collector was considered the worst kind of sinner. Then we find the story of the rich young ruler who asks Jesus what he must do to inherit eternal life. Jesus tells him to sell all that he has and follow him. Distraught, the rich young ruler walks away, unwilling to part with his riches. Jesus then says, "How hard it is for those who are rich to enter the kingdom of God" (Luke 18:24). His hearers are shocked. During Jesus's day, it was assumed that riches were God's blessing. So in response to Jesus's words they say, "Well, if the rich are going to have trouble getting into heaven, then who can be saved?" Jesus responds, "What is impossible with humanity is possible with God" (see Luke 18:26–27).

The stage is now set for the story of Zacchaeus in Luke chapter 19. Not only is Zacchaeus a tax collector, but he is the *chief* tax collector, and he is quite rich. Culturally, Zacchaeus has a snowball's chance in hell to experience salvation. But Jesus singles Zacchaeus out of the crowd and invites himself to lunch. What happens at that lunch is unknown, but Zacchaeus comes away a changed man, promising to repay everyone he defrauded. One way of viewing this is to consider that Jesus gave Zacchaeus the gift of nonjudgment, engaging the tax collector without condemnation. Perhaps Zacchaeus is given the psychological and spiritual freedom to change his way of being because Jesus looks on him with the eyes of innocence.

Making Judgments versus Being Judgmental

A tricky thing about judgmental behavior is that we have to make judgments in order to survive. So what is the difference between making judgments—that is, everyday evaluations of our surroundings—and being judgmental? In an article in *Psychology Today*, Dr. Gregg Henriques, a professor of psychology at James Madison University, describes *making judgments* as forming opinions or decisions based on careful thought and *being judgmental* as the tendency to be overly critical in unhelpful ways.

> Someone is being judgmental when their judgments are power-driven, unempathetic, based on their own idiosyncratic values or tastes, overly based on other people's character, and are closed, shallow, and pessimistic, and ultimately have the consequence of making the other person feel problematically diminished.[2]

Being judgmental is certainly not childlike! Returning to Luke chapter 19, we see that Jesus is not fooled by Zacchaeus; he is aware of his fraudulent ways. But he looks past these to the part of Zacchaeus created in the image of God. We are invited to do the same. This way of seeing one another taps into our potential to respond not in habitual ways, but with love, kindness, and justice.

Just as Jesus chooses to engage Zacchaeus with love, we can choose the same. We can choose to move forward in an overly judgmental way that repels love, kindness, and justice, or we can make judgments with the eyes of innocence and move forward, engaging in love, compassion, empathy, and kindness. In *God of Becoming and Relationship: The Dynamic Nature of Process Theology*, Rabbi Bradley Shavit Artson writes:

> To love someone is to become vulnerable to his or her choices. It is to suffer another's pain, and to exalt in the lover's triumph. It is to want to be steadily a partner and helper, and to sometimes be hurt by the partner's rejection or bad choices.[3]

Contemporary theologian Matthew Fox recalls Thomas Aquinas, thirteenth-century theologian, who said, "The first effect of love is melting."

> The first thing love does is to melt. That's the opposite of freezing. We can be frozen with anger, resentment, hurt [prejudice,

judgment, etc.], and we've got to do some melting. Melting is always movement. I think that's a way to look at forgiveness too, as melting.[4]

Having judgmental thinking melt away with love can occur suddenly, in places we least expect. That's what happened to Kristen, a friend of a member of the church I served in California. Kristen was in her car, sitting in traffic, when she looked at the car beside her and made a series of snap judgments: a poor and ignorant family; poorly parented, too, since five kids, dirty and raggedly dressed, were piled in the back with no seat belts on. She looked again, and a little girl stared at her and smiled a smile that, as she put it, "lit up her crowded back seat and spread across the pavement right into my car, into my toes, up through my body and into my heart." Suddenly, Kristen's judgments melted away and she said,

> I learned from that moment. It is human nature for us to make judgments about people, even if they are only in our own brains and we never say or do anything to let the other person know.
>
> I know that I am not alone in thinking that I am an open-minded person who does not make decisions about people based on race or religion. And I don't think I'm a bad person, or a person who thinks horrible thoughts about people all the time, but I am going to make a concerted effort not to make those same decisions based on outer appearance. All it took was a moment at a traffic light. I will remember how [that little girl] made me feel, and I'm interested to see how her smile will change the way I think of and interact with other people in this world we all share.

To become like a child, to see with the eyes of innocence, is to dramatically change the way we interact with one another—and with ourselves.

Turning the Eyes of Innocence on Ourselves

One of the most difficult people to see with the eyes of innocence is our own selves. We know our history and tend to believe it defines us. We know our habits and faults all too well. We also know those moments when we say about ourselves, "That's not me," reflecting a knowledge of the core or true self that is at the heart of us, often buried under the false self and roles we learn to play. Turning the eyes of innocence on ourselves allows us to reconnect with our authentic selves, to use as a guide, as true north.

A friend of mine tells of counseling a woman who suffered from depression and substance abuse. She had lived through a difficult childhood and several abusive marriages. My friend asked her to tell him about a season of her life that was good and life-affirming. She couldn't come up with anything. He asked her to recall a month, or even a week, when she had felt good. Nothing. He then asked her if she remembered a *moment* of clarity, grace, true self. She thought for a moment and finally said, "When I was standing at the altar at my first wedding, I suddenly knew this man was not right for me, and I should just walk out. But I couldn't do it."

My friend listened to more of her story and then asked her, "Have there been other moments like that?" Slowly the woman began to remember moments of insight and wisdom, when her true self had let itself be known. She began to realize that this part of her, though deeply buried under self-recrimination and self-medication, was still there, still very much alive. One step at a time, she began to trust that voice, that self, and to see herself without self-judgment, and her healing began to unfold.

When we come home to ourselves—call it what you will: true self, big self, the image of God, soul, inner light, the spark of the Divine, Christ-consciousness—it is the "us" that is beyond history, culture, social context, and time. When we view ourselves with the eyes of innocence, we tap into the deep river of our soul and invite it to spring forth where our true self is made manifest in our daily lives. As Parker J. Palmer says, the soul "never stops calling us back to our birthright integrity."[5]

Let me share one final story, from an unknown author, that gets to the heart of the childlike ability to see with innocent eyes.

> We were the only family with children in the restaurant. I sat Erik in a high chair and noticed everyone was quietly eating and talking. Suddenly, Erik squealed with glee and said, "Hi there." He pounded his fat baby hands on the high chair tray. His eyes were wide with excitement and his mouth was bared in a toothless grin. He wriggled and giggled with merriment. I looked around and saw the source of his merriment. It was a man with a tattered rag of a

coat; dirty, greasy, and worn. His pants were baggy, with a zipper at half-mast, and his toes poked out of would-be shoes. His shirt was dirty and his hair was uncombed and unwashed. His whiskers were too short to be called a beard and his nose was so varicose it looked like a road map. We were too far from him to smell, but I was sure he smelled. His hands waved and flapped on loose wrists. "Hi there, baby; hi there, big boy. I see ya, buster," the man said to Erik. My husband and I exchanged looks, "What do we do?" Erik continued to laugh and answer, "Hi, hi there." Everyone in the restaurant noticed and looked at us and then at the man. The old geezer was creating a nuisance with my beautiful baby.

Our meal came and the man began shouting from across the room, "Do ya know patty cake? Do you know peek-a-boo? Hey, look, he knows peek-a-boo." Nobody thought the old man was cute. He was obviously drunk. My husband and I were embarrassed. We ate in silence; all except for Erik, who was running through his repertoire for the admiring skid-row bum, who, in turn, reciprocated with his cute comments. We finally got through the meal and headed for the door. My husband went to pay the check and told me to meet him in the parking lot. The old man sat poised between me and the door. "Lord, just let me out of here before he speaks to me or Erik," I prayed. As I drew closer to the man, I turned my back trying to sidestep him and avoid any air he might be breathing. As I did, Erik leaned over my arm, reaching with both arms in a baby's "pick-me-up" position. Before I could stop him, Erik had propelled himself from my arms to the man's. Suddenly a very old smelly man and a very young baby consummated their love relationship. Erik in an act of total trust, love, and submission laid his tiny head upon the man's ragged shoulder. The man's eyes closed, and I saw tears hover beneath his lashes. His aged hands full of grime, pain, and hard labor gently, so gently, cradled my baby's bottom and stroked his back.

No two beings have ever loved so deeply for so short a time. I stood awestruck. The old man rocked and cradled Erik in his arms for a moment, and then his eyes opened and set squarely on mine. He said in a firm, commanding voice, "You take care of this baby."

Somehow I managed, "I will," from a throat that contained a stone. He pried Erik from his chest—unwillingly, longingly, as though he was in pain. I received my baby, and the man said, "God bless you, ma'am, you've given me my Christmas gift." I said nothing more than a muttered thanks.

With Erik in my arms, I ran for the car. My husband was wondering why I was crying and holding Erik so tightly, and why I was saying, "My God, my God, forgive me." I had just witnessed Christ's love shown through the innocence of a tiny child who saw no sin, who made no judgment; a child who saw a soul, and a mother who saw a suit of clothes. I was a Christian who was blind, holding a child who was not. I felt it was God asking, "Are you willing to share your son for a moment?" when He shared His for all eternity. The ragged old man, unwittingly, had reminded me, "To enter the kingdom of God, we must become as little children."[6]

Practices

A Pair of Glasses

One of the most important pieces of wisdom we gained in the twentieth century is the notion that we can never fully have an unbiased perspective. We are always looking through a pair of glasses, if not several. Our culture, language, social context, and personal experience give us lenses through which we see, interpret, and judge life. Although we can never see completely objectively, we can become aware of the beliefs, values, and judgments through which we "see" others and the world around us.

Put on a pair of reading glasses or sunglasses, and call to mind a person or a situation that is difficult or troubling for you. In the silence and quiet, allow all the judgments, feelings, and "seeing" of this person or situation to come into your awareness without judging them or criticizing yourself. Simply notice them and acknowledge them. Then ask yourself, as you remove the glasses slowly from your eyes:

Through what lenses am I seeing this person or situation?

What values, experiences, assumptions, or beliefs of mine are making me see this person or situation in particular ways?

Can I let go of some of these judgments and assumptions, and see this person or situation as they are or as it is?

How does changing the way I see shift how I feel about this person or situation? How might I act on that shift?

A Conversation with Your True Self

Set aside 20 to 30 minutes when you will not be interrupted. First, call to mind some of the critical and judgmental voices in your life. Can you identify the sources of these voices? It is likely you will find some combination of judgmental voices from parents, other family members, important people, culture, and religion. It is important first to become aware of these voices and where they come from because they can often be heard as the voice of God or the true self.

Now that you have become aware of the sources of judgment in your life, ask your true self what it would like to say to you.

Sit quietly and listen for what arises, and then write down what you feel your true self might be saying.

When you come to the end of a thought, ask your true self again, "What would you like to say to me?"

As you record this dialogue, continue to ask questions of your true self as they come to mind.

In your daily life, listen for the sound of your true voice, and its wisdom.

How is it different from the critical voices or cultural voices?

How is it inviting you to think and act differently?

5 The Truth of a Tantrum

DISCERNING THE GIFTS IN DESIRE AND EMOTION

You have nothing infinite except your soul's love and desire.

CATHERINE OF SIENNA

When we can uncover our deepest longings for intimacy, pleasure, creativity, and self-understanding, life yields illumination and happiness. Far from being a burden, our desires themselves become a path to blessing.

RABBI IRWIN KULA

While reading the paper outside a local coffee shop, I was privy to a double tantrum thrown by a boy and his grandfather. The boy struggled in his grandfather's arms, wailing in inconsolable anguish, "I don't want it!" The grandfather, jaw firmly set as he held on to the screaming boy, sat down next to the grandmother and explained, "He got the bagel he wanted and now he wants to get a different one, and I won't let him!"

What is a child if not incredibly willful? A child is a bundle of desires unbridled, worn on the sleeve, expressed, acted out without thought. Is this what Jesus had in mind when he urged us to become like children? Is he inviting us into a willful existence, expressing and acting out everything we feel and desire? My first reaction to this is no. This goes against the grain of Jesus's teachings. His words—"The first shall be last and the last first," "Take up your cross and follow me," "Whoever loses their life will gain it," and "Not my will, but yours be done"—all paint a picture of someone who is not willful, who puts the desires of others before his own. But, as we have seen, Jesus invites us to become childlike with adult awareness, compassion, and choice. What would it mean for us if we included—and embraced—our desires and emotions in that process?

Playing All the Keys

We live out our lives much like playing the piano. A piano keyboard is composed of white keys and black keys. The white keys are the natural notes—those of the major C scale—and are generally thought to be pleasing notes to our ears. The black keys are the sharps and flats—notes outside the major C scale. While not necessarily unpleasing to our ears, sharps and flats are moodier than natural notes; they often deliver the tone and texture of music. As young children, we pound out our desires and emotions willfully, using every key indiscriminately. *I'm hungry! I'm mad! I'm hurt! I want that! I'm so happy! Gimme, gimme, gimme!* Reacting to our cacophony, parents, family, and, to a lesser degree, our community, give us piano lessons.

"We don't like to hear anger, so don't use those keys. Use these keys instead."

"Here's how you say, 'Thank you, Mommy.'"

"Oh no, not so loud! You want to play soft. You don't want to draw attention to yourself."

"Don't talk to me with those notes! Don't ever play that again!"

Day after day, year after year, we are taught to play the piano of our souls in a socially acceptable way until that's the only way we know how to play. Of course we can rebel against parental and cultural pressures and find our own way to play, but often this style is not really our own, either. It is more reaction—an expression of a negatively formed sense of self rather than a self freely chosen. Whether playing through acquiescence or rebellion, we play with a diminished number of keys, within a certain range of volume, and in only certain styles of music. We limit the range and growth of our souls.

Reading Our Tantrums

Well-known American psychologist James Hillman describes his acorn theory in his powerful book *The Soul's Code: In Search of Character and Calling*. He points to the idea that our souls know something more about who we are than we do. Just as an acorn grows into an oak tree, our soul is an "acorn" that contains the essence of our true self and yearns to be brought to fruition in our lives. The ancient Romans referred to this aspect of soul as our "genius," the Greeks as our "daimon," and some branches of Christianity depicted it as our "guardian angel." Hillman says that our soul's unique character is often revealed to us more clearly in childhood. Tantrum-like behavior, rather than being indicative of a troubled child, is often a sign of deeper desires that reflect the true self.

Hillman tells this story about renowned violinist Yehudi Menuhin when he was but a child:

> Before Yehudi was four he frequently heard the concertmaster (first violinist) Louis Persinger break into a solo passage as little Yehudi sat with his parents up in the gallery of the Curran Theatre. "During one such performance I asked my parents if I might have a violin for my fourth birthday and Louis Persinger to teach me to play it." His wish was granted, it seems, when he was given, by a family friend, a toy violin made of metal with metal strings. "I burst into sobs, threw it on the ground and would have nothing more to do with it." ...
>
> Let us consider that little Yehudi's daimon refused to be treated as a child, despite the fact that the boy himself was only four. The daimon threw the fit, demanding the real thing, for playing the violin is not playing with a toy.[1]

Could it be that our own tantrum-like expressions—our deep longings, strong desires, and urgent impulses—communicate the unlived parts of our true self and deserve to be listened to with patience, compassion, and understanding?

Listening for the Sharps and Flats

The repression of unruly and unacceptable desires, thoughts, and emotions does not rid us of them. They still play deep within us, and they find ways of showing up in our lives. Perhaps we learned to always be upbeat and unselfish—only playing the natural major C scale notes—but others begin to hear us sounding angry, bitter, choked—the sounds of sharps and flats creeping through.

Sometimes the unacceptable or less important parts of us that we have repressed, or refuse to express, play without our control, contradicting who we think we are.

My freshmen year in college I spent a good bit of the latter part of the first semester drawing one-of-a-kind, individual Christmas cards for my wonderful new friends. My grades reflected how much time I spent on the cards instead of my studies. My sophomore year I took a Studio Experience in Drawing class and after a few weeks the professor wanted me to become an art major. I refused because I was going into the ministry. But even in my ministry I would spend a great deal of time making creative posters for upcoming youth events.

After resigning from the church and applying to a doctoral program, I headed off to Germany to study my research language. When I was not accepted for the PhD program, I waited tables, began writing a novel, and started painting. I sold my first painting, and then another, and another. My sister had been "the artist" in the family, but could it be that that's who I was, too?

When I looked back on my life, I suddenly realized how much those creative, artistic notes kept playing in me, but I had minimized them. I soon found another pastoral position, but part time. I am a pastor *and* an artist, and I wanted to give the artist room to develop and emerge.

But even as we grow spiritually and reclaim parts of ourselves, we may find it difficult to change our habitual ways of playing our souls. We tend to return to playing the old familiar tunes of our lives that we learned from others. It takes courage to play our own tune.

Playing Our Own Tune

A woman named Mary came to see me for spiritual direction. Mary worked in a corporate setting and made good money, but something was missing in her life. I asked her what she loved about her childhood. Mary began to talk about how she loved learning and going to school. After school, she would often play the teacher, arraying her dolls in rows like they were in a classroom.

Mary began to talk about her desire to become a teacher, something she'd been thinking about for quite a while. She sat up straight in her chair, her eyes brightened, and her voice and body language became animated. But suddenly Mary stopped talking and slumped back in her chair. Her eyes dropped and she said meekly, "I should just be thankful for what I have."

I mirrored back to her what I had just witnessed, and asked her, "Whose voice is it that says you should just be thankful for what you have?" I watched her eyes grow wide in recognition, and she exclaimed, "My mother!" Mary began to see how much she had made her mother's wishes more important than her own; she had even equated her mother's voice with God's. Mary decided she had played her mother's notes long enough; it was time to play the notes that were her own.

As these two stories show, our repressed, "unacceptable" desires and feelings are often the marks of wounds in need of healing. These desires and feeling may also reveal parts of our true self in need of being welcomed and lived. Our unacknowledged, unaccepted, untreated wounds, as well as our unlived strengths, gifts, and soul's purpose, diminish our capacity to love ourselves and love others. We cannot love deeply, work for justice, and be who we really are without the full range of keys.

To become childlike is to embrace the full range of keys of our souls, with awareness, compassion, and choice, hearing and playing all the desires and emotions within us like an accomplished pianist. In doing so we become whole.

Becoming Whole: Reconciling with All Our Emotions

Wholeness is a biblical word found in the Gospel of Matthew. When Jesus says, "Be perfect as your heavenly Father is perfect" (5:48), he is instructing us to be whole. The Greek word *teleios*, usually translated as "perfect," is a much more complex word, meaning completeness, wholeness, fullness, maturity, oneness. Becoming whole is the result of becoming aware of all the emotions, thoughts, and desires playing within us, and bringing them into God's gracious presence in prayer. We need to admit to all our desires and emotions: (1) admit, as in confess and acknowledge to ourselves, and God, what is real in us; and (2) admit, as in allow those desires and emotions entrance into our awareness. As we admit all these aspects of ourselves to God, we find God healing us, honing our desires down to the deepest, truest desires within us, making us whole.

Psychology and religion authors Barry and Ann Ulanov write in their book *Primary Speech: A Psychology of Prayer*,

> God hears all the voices that speak out of us—our vocal prayer, the prayer said in our minds, the unvoiced longing rising from our hearts, the many voices of which we are not conscious but which cry out eloquently.... We begin to hear the self we actually are emerging out of our shadow selves, our counterfeit selves, our pretended selves. We become aware of what is in us, the best and the worst....
>
> Our best parts, if left unlived, can be as poisonous as our worst, if left unhealed.... If prayer is ... the most direct line of communication to our interior reality, then every denial of that reality, every judgment or retreat from it that shuts off access to it is a serious diminishing of ourselves. It is, in fact, a kind of refusal to be.[2]

The inability to accept and acknowledge one's feelings was portrayed comically and poignantly by actor Jim Carrey in the movie *Me, Myself, and Irene*. Playing the role of a motorcycle cop who refuses to acknowledge the hurt he feels by his wife's infidelity and the way others mistreat him, Carrey's character splits into two personalities. One is good and kind; the other is mean and nasty. The movie turns on the battles between the two. But as the movie progresses, Carrey's character discovers that the mean side of his personality would not have come to the fore if he had been willing to allow himself to feel hurt, anger, sadness, and grief, and if he had allowed himself to express his feelings to his wife and others. By voicing what he really feels and experiences, the two personalities begin to merge and become whole again.

My own story of restoring a part of myself by becoming aware of repressed desires is less dramatic, but still significant. In seminary I performed in a campus production of *Thurber's Carnival*, playing a role that asked me to progressively get angrier and angrier. In the final scene, I was given carte blanche to erupt with white-hot, volcanic ire. My fellow amateur thespians were envious of my role—it sounded so cathartic!—but I found it quite difficult. Anger had not been acceptable in my family. In college I remember proudly telling a friend that I *never* got mad. I had the mistaken notion that a Christian wasn't supposed to get angry. I had learned to shove anger—and other so-called negative emotions—under the carpet. The director of the play eventually had to express his anger at *me* because I wasn't being angry enough! By opening night, with lots of practice, I was able to express my anger. My seminary friends said, "Wow, we've never seen that part of you!" It felt amazingly good.

Embracing Our Emotions Willingly Rather Than Willfully

Just *expressing* anger or hurt or grief isn't enough. Some psychologists have encouraged the expression of everything one feels: Don't hold back, just let it out. But this can cause a great deal of hurt and pain. There is a profound difference between expressing every emotion and desire and *being aware of*, feeling, and praying with and through our emotions and longings.

Becoming aware of our emotions, observing them in contemplation without acting on them, offers a profound freedom. "In the experience of quiet," writes Gerald May, "one begins to observe that there is always a space between feeling and response, between the impulse and the action. Within this space there is a great freedom for choice."[3] Within that space, God is very present.

Children admit everything about their world and experience. When they are hungry, they cry out. When they are hurt or sad, they feel it, show the expression on their faces, let tears come. When they are happy, they embody it, dancing with delight. So, too, as adults we are invited to admit internally, feel bodily, all that is real within us.

How do we do this without pushing people away with childish—not childlike—volcanic emotional eruptions? Gerald May, in his book *Will and*

Spirit, provides a helpful distinction: We must be willing, rather than willful, to embrace our emotions and desires. What would it mean for us to attend to all our desires and emotions willingly rather than willfully, with our whole selves?

Jesus practices this in the Garden of Gethsemane, as he struggles with the knowledge of his pending death and the cruel and violent manner in which it will be played out (Matthew 26:36–56). In his prayer he lays bare all his desires and emotions. He pleads, asks if there is any other way, sweats drops of blood, according to some manuscripts. Every desire and emotion is brought to awareness, admitted, allowed to exist, voiced, brought to God. Due to the length and anguished nature of this prayer, I do not hesitate to call it a tantrum of sorts. But in this place of prayer, where Jesus acknowledges all his desires and emotions, he finds the freedom to respond, not willfully, but willingly.

Uncovering Our Yearnings

Another key to willingly embracing our emotions is identifying what our soul's true desires are, and recognizing the way our mind is often at odds with our soul. Contemporary life coach Martha Beck advises that our minds are conditioned to think in narrow little patterns, usually established by our families and our culture. The soul tells us what we want and need, while the mind tells us what we *think* we want and need.

> The soul knows, "I want freedom from worry," and the mind thinks, "I want to win the lottery." The soul knows, "I want to feel connected with all things," and the mind translates that to, "I need the perfect romantic soul mate to make me feel connected." The soul is always right.[4]

To get to the root of things, Beck says, it can be helpful to pick up a pencil and write down everything you "want." Then on a clean piece of paper, start writing down what you "yearn for."

> You'll find yourself coming up with things that didn't appear on your first list, which was made mostly by your mind. We want cars—we yearn for freedom and mobility. We want hot sex—we yearn for intimacy. We want to be beautiful—we yearn for total

self-acceptance. As you list the things your soul yearns for, let go of the need to figure out how they might be fulfilled…. Allow yourself to be okay with not knowing, for the present moment, how the universe intends to fulfill your soul's desires.[5]

Journaling in this way was very helpful for me in identifying the root causes of my emotions. A few hours before the beginning of my final three-week session in the diploma program in the Art of Spiritual Direction at San Francisco Theological Seminary, I was in a coffee shop in San Anselmo, California, writing in my journal. Unexpectedly, I found myself quite agitated about the program. I did not want to be around a bunch of people showing off their progress in spiritual development, demonstrating how much they had improved since the previous January. My agitation surprised me because I genuinely liked the people in the program. I was tempted to repress these unruly feelings, but instead I started journaling about them and I soon found a torrent of anger, disappointment, and unrealized desires pouring out on the pages of my journal. I let God have it! Much like my experience in *Thurber's Carnival*, I relished feeling the anger, and becoming aware of the myriad desires at work in me.

As I lashed out at God, complaining about my lot in life, I began to see how much of the responsibility for my life's direction fell squarely on my own shoulders. My resistance to interacting with my fellow students reflected my resistance to acknowledging my own seemingly unacceptable desires and longings, a resistance born out of fear.

By giving myself the freedom to recognize and articulate my feelings and desires, I found a growing willingness to see what was really going on inside me. I was feeling pressure to have my own spiritual life all neat and tidy, when in fact I was sailing through stormy waters. Admitting all that was within me into my awareness allowed me to embrace that reality. The ensuing gift of freedom resulted in a greater openness and a willingness to navigate the stormy seas of my own spiritual journey without judgment. I found that accepting where I was transformed my attitude toward being with the other students. My agitation just disappeared. My tantrum revealed my deeper intentions, and helped me to manifest the desires that I had been resisting out of fear.

The emotions and desires we experience are the indicators of the motions and directions of our lives. Contrary to the notion that the self is unchanging, the self is constantly in motion. The self is not static, but ever-changing and evolving. Theologian and professor of Christian spirituality Philip Sheldrake invites us to see our emotions and desires as the stuff of spiritual transformation when he writes,

> Being people of desire also means that we live within a condition of constant change rather than experienc[ing] occasional changes from one static situation to another. Our spiritual journeys are essentially stories of continual transition. In this way, desire may become a metaphor for transformation.[6]

Sharing Your Desiring Heart with God

Have you noticed that a child rarely throws a tantrum in isolation? It is always for another to hear. If we listen deeply enough, all the desires and emotions in us cry out for another to hear—the One who is always there. As Ann and Barry Ulanov point out, "All [the voices in us], like arrows, point to one aim: the Other who hears us. God thus becomes the primary focus of our prayerful primary speech."[7]

The recognition, acceptance, and embrace of all that we find within ourselves reflect the recognition, acceptance, and embrace of God. The Ulanovs write:

> Our experience in prayer tells us that God wants us and accepts us as we are. What is not wanted is outward compliance with the rules while inwardly we chafe in rebellion and grievance. No deals. No bargaining. No saying that if we yield here, then God must yield there. No righteous puffing up over how splendidly we keep the rules. No guaranteed rewards. Our prayers tell us in every possible way that God wants a desiring heart, a glad heart, an angry heart, a fearful heart—our heart just as it is, freely given and freely exposed.[8]

That sounds like the heart of a child playing on all the keys. If we are willing, in prayer and community, God will teach us to play well on the piano of our souls.

Practices

Throw a Fit

Set aside at least 30 minutes when you are alone. Think of something that really bothers you or has disappointed or angered you and give yourself permission to throw a fit. Even if you don't feel like you have something to throw a fit about, begin acting and see what emotions or memories surface.

Involving your body in this exercise helps access feelings that might not emerge if it were just an intellectual exercise. It is important to do this in such a way that you, others, and property will be protected and safe. For example, you might close the door to your bedroom and throw or punch pillows as you vocalize your feelings.

Once you have allowed yourself to say, feel, and embody what you usually keep below the surface, take the time to journal or record your experience and your reflections on it.

Throwing a fit may feel awkward, if not childish, but it provides a way for you to recognize and experience the myriad complaints, disappointments, and laments that exist within you, as well as the underlying and often conflicting desires and longings. The key is becoming aware of what lies within you, and prayerfully reflecting on what you find.

What Do You Want Me to Do for You?

Jesus is portrayed in the Gospels as asking others, "What do you want me to do for you?" Ignatius of Loyola, the founder of the Society of Jesus (better known as the Jesuits), made this a key component of spiritual formation and prayers of discernment.

Set aside 30 minutes in a comfortable place where you will not be interrupted. Prayerfully imagine God asking you, "What do you want me to do for you?" After your initial response, keep responding to this question and delve more deeply into the heart of your desires and longings. What is it that you *really* want?

When you have allowed your true self to open up and express these desires, be gentle in your response. Don't criticize or judge, but simply treasure any realizations or new knowledge of your deepest self. Hold them quietly in your heart as you go about your daily life, and see what they might blossom into.

6 Change the Way You Think

RECLAIMING BEGINNER'S MIND (OLD DOGS THRIVE ON NEW TRICKS!)

> When you've got an answer, it's time
> to find better questions.
>
> RABBI IRWIN KULA'S MOTHER

Kids think with their brains cracked wide
open; becoming an adult, I've decided,
is only a slow sewing shut.

JODI PICOULT

My gift for Dezi, Julie's daughter, for her sixth birthday, was a ukulele. It came with a chart diagramming the finger patterns for the chords. Eventually, I thought, Dezi would learn the chords, perform some simple songs, and play confidently in front of other people. Fifteen minutes later, on the drive to her birthday dinner, strapped into her car seat, Dezi started strumming the ukulele and, on the spot, made up a song about her day. Her mother and I looked at each other with astonishment. She didn't play the correct chords but she found a pattern of sorts, stayed on key, and most of her verses rhymed!

Children are like sponges when it comes to learning. Adults, on the other hand—many of us anyway—are like bricks. We know what we need to know and aren't about to change our minds now. But that approach, whether intentional or unconscious, diminishes who we are. Jesus's urging us to become like children encourages us to reopen our minds to learning and growth, and to fully participate in our potential as God's creation.

Helpful Routine or Mind-numbing Rut?

As adults we mostly follow learned habits—mental, emotional, and physical—and we become slaves to our routines. On the one hand, our routines allow us to get through the day's tasks in a smooth and organized way—wake up at 6 a.m., dress, get the kids fed, out the door, and in the car by 8 a.m., and be at work by 9 a.m. Our routines—mental and physical—help us cut down on stress: Who among us would want to learn to tie our shoes again each morning, or learn how to use a computer all over again? On the other hand, routines can dull our senses, encourage a one-track mind, and soon enough we find ourselves in a rut. Ruts allow us to turn off our minds and tune out the world outside our daily patterns. But they also keep us thinking, feeling, seeing, and believing in the same, familiar, narrow ways. When routines of the heart, mind, and spirit settle in, they prevent us from being open to new information and experiences. Learning becomes diminished, if it has not ceased altogether, and we wonder why our lives seem flat and meaningless.

But recent research on the plasticity of the brain provides convincing evidence that if we have fallen into a mental or emotional rut, we can change the way we think. In childhood our brains experience what neuroscientists call "critical periods" of brain development, when simple exposure to ideas, reading and writing, motor skills, and language make an imprint on the neurological mapping of the brain. This is why children are able to learn so quickly, easily—hungrily. At a certain point, however, each critical period shuts down in order to preserve what has been learned. In extreme cases, some neuroscientists suggest that learning ability can atrophy, as in cases of diminished memory and mental acuity in seniors. But research shows that certain conditions—focusing our attention, contemplation, challenging our patterns—can make the brain return to that state of intense learning. We can learn to think, feel, and behave differently.

Finding Inner Wisdom through Beginner's Mind

To become like a child means to reclaim our child's mind—to be curious and continue to learn, grow, and change. Zen Buddhists call this "beginner's mind," when we let go of our habits, routines, patterns, prejudices, and preconceptions, and engage the world around us with a sense of openness and receptivity. The endless repetition by children of the question "Why?" demonstrates beginner's mind. As adults, achieving beginner's mind requires that we cultivate the desire, curiosity, and intention to learn new things in order to overcome entrenched behaviors, ideas, attitudes, and emotions. Old dogs can learn new tricks—and unlearn the old ones!

The story of Abraham and Sarah in the book of Genesis points to this capability. Abraham and Sarah were advanced in age when God's call came: Pack up the U-Haul and go to a land I will show you. A new start, a new adventure, leaving what was known and familiar for the unknown and unfamiliar. But one of the surprising things about this story is the Hebrew translation of the words Abraham heard: "*Go to yourself*, leave your land, your father's house and go to a land I will show you … and you will be a source of blessing."[1]

Something powerful occurs when we search for new wisdom, whether our search is external or internal. When we go to ourselves, when we listen deeply to what is within, we will leave our ruts behind and find a land that becomes our own, even though it is not known at the start. Going within and leaving what they know and the traditions of their time, Abraham and his wife Sarah, not without considerable challenge and anguish, become the source of several nations, and a blessing to many. The promise of this beginner's mind is blessing for ourselves, others, and the world.

My friend Gary exercises beginner's mind in his daily commute to work. Each day he takes a different route to his office. He's discovered that this makes him more attentive overall; he's found new cafes, restaurants, and unique stores, and it prepares him to be creative and productive at work. Taking many routes to the same destination has helped Gary see that he can take many different paths with his colleagues, in grappling with the challenges and crises they all face together, to reach their common goals.

Seeing the World Anew Each Moment

Adopting beginner's mind is easier said than done. Recently I went skiing for two days with Julie and Dezi. At the beginning of the second day, Dezi wanted to make a plan. She came up with three things. Here's what she wrote:

ske day plans
- ske run akros the stret
- ske run bi ske skol
- c is fort

For those of you who can't read six-year-old, her plans were to ski the runs at the lift across the street from where we were staying, take the ski run next to the ski school, and see the ice fort before we had to leave to get back to fulfill other responsibilities.

We had a great day. Dezi improved her skiing, I stole away long enough to get in some powder runs, and her hot chocolate afterward was good even after she tried salt in it to see how that tasted.

But when we got to item number 3, the ice fort, it was closed. Dezi was very disappointed, but I was thinking, "Well, we can get an early start home," so I started walking back toward the car. But Dezi was upset and wanted to see if there was another entrance, or another ice fort we didn't know about. So we walked around—but, of course, there was only one ice fort.

Dezi was going slowly, and I became impatient. I found myself saying internally, "Don't let her get us distracted. Don't give in to her disappointment. Let's stick with the plan and go home." Just as I was about to say something to Julie, Dezi started climbing up a ten-foot hill of snow made by snowplows and snowblowers. "Now we'll never get out of here," I thought. But then I caught myself and became present to my thinking. Why was I so worried about time? We had plenty of time! I began to see that I simply wanted things to go the way I had planned—even though I didn't write my plan on a piece of paper.

Letting go of all those thoughts and expectations, I found a new freedom to be in the moment, and a great idea popped into my head! I ran around to the other side of the hill of snow and climbed up to meet Dezi on top.

For the next twenty minutes we turned the hill of snow into our playground. We hopped and flopped and danced in the snow. I threw Dezi into a big, soft drift of powder. We took turns sprawling in the snow at the top of the hill and then rolling all the way down to the sidewalk, covered completely in snow. We laughed so hard. Afterward, I realized how easy it is for me to stay within a narrow range of thinking, behaving, and feeling that might be known and comfortable, but is inhibiting and often unfairly judgmental of the situation and of others. All it took was a moment for me to see it differently, to let go of what was "supposed" to happen and let what might be reveal itself.

Rethinking Our Lives

Meditation practitioner Patricia Hart Clifford, in her insightful little book *Sitting Still: An Encounter with Christian Zen*, describes the profound change beginner's mind had on her in the middle of her life, through the practice of meditation. She left the church in her college years, and had dabbled in Zen meditation, but eventually become involved in an Episcopal church. Her longing for the beauty of stillness that she experienced in nature, and in meditation, prompted her to register for a weeklong retreat in which she and others would meditate for six hours each day in silence. At the end of the retreat she wrote, "Real change takes more than meditating for a specified amount of time every day. It takes a practice of nonjudgmental attention to both inner and outer experience that comes to permeate everything we do."[2]

In reflecting on her own experience, and the experience of several others from the retreat, she found that old patterns had become a narrow and anxious prism through which she viewed her life. Her life had been circumscribed by patterns of seeking to meet cultural and familial expectations, and to be liked and seen as acceptable. But engaging beginner's mind through her regular meditation practice revitalized her sense of self, freeing her to be who she is, and set her on a path of trust and hopefulness.

The story of Patricia Hart Clifford points to the phenomenon of what Westerners call the "midlife crisis." In Western culture, a midlife crisis may set us on a path to greater openness and transformation. It can provide a season of rethinking our lives. Familial roles, cultural expectations, and corporate myths lose their appeal, as we find ourselves experiencing deeper longings for meaning and purpose. A deeper, truer sense of self emerges and is the impetus for many to unlearn much of what they have learned, and to explore new ways of being in the world.

Finding Beginner's Mind in Crisis

When change is forced on us, beginner's mind can help us find opportunity in crisis. Divorce, which makes us reexamine our lives as individuals rather than one of a pair, may inspire a reconsideration of authentic personal likes and dislikes. Corporate downsizing and job loss may help us connect with our true calling. As our physical capacities begin to wane with age, this may prod us to find new hobbies and ways of enjoying our leisure time.

A good friend, Brandon, and his wife had moved to Chicago. He had been offered a new job, and though they hated the thought of leaving California, they both felt it was the right thing to do. But soon it became clear that his wife was unhappy in the Windy City; the cold winter winds of Chicago seemed to blow all year long. After much prayer and discernment they decided to move to Seattle, Washington, and things seemed to improve. Then, unexpectedly, Brandon's wife said she was leaving him, and she returned that week to her ex-husband.

Brandon's life and world were completely thrown off center and upside down. He said it was as if one day, it was him and his wife, and the next day it was this man who didn't know if he could trust his feelings, instincts, or intuitions, and a woman he hardly recognized at all.

Brandon entered a long season of starting over from scratch—engaging beginner's mind—and taking the time for quiet and meditation, listening to his deep longings and to what seemed most real and true. He set his sights on letting go of expectations and assumptions that seemed foreign to his soul. Brandon returned to Chicago, to a job well suited to his gifts and passions, and he moved into a neighborhood that suited his tastes. He realized how much of himself he had sacrificed or left fallow in his previous relationships and he began to live closer to his own truth. As Brandon slowly emerged from his devastating loss, others began to notice his energy, sense of humor, and solid sense of self. Brandon's boss arranged a meeting with a woman friend of his, and the two immediately hit it off. Brandon and Angie have been married for fifteen years now and are doing well.

Willingness to Change Our Minds

The Christian Scriptures use the Greek word *metanoia* to indicate spiritual change and transformation. *Metanoia* (*meta*, "beyond," and *noia*, "mind") means to turn around, go beyond, change your mind. This ability to change, turn, transform, go beyond, and reimagine—exercising beginner's mind—lies at the heart of a vibrant spiritual life. Certainty discourages, if not disparages, going beyond. Post–World War II writer and poet Edmond Jabés writes in *The Book of Questions*,

> Certainty is the region of death; uncertainty is the valley of life. Once we can liberate ourselves from the tyranny of needing to be certain, it becomes possible to take, as William Blake wrote, "eternal delight in the undecidable."[3]

Our desire for the comforts of certainty can pervade every aspect of our lives without our realizing it. My pastor friend Gail recently posted on her Facebook page:

> So today at the Walt Disney Family Museum, there were several quotes from Walt that referenced the moldable, changeable, and shapeable qualities of Disneyland and the Disney ventures.
>
> I hate the way I take every enjoyable thing and try to relate it to or compare it to the institutional church. Nonetheless, I was wondering why we have gotten into this mode of measuring the success of the church via what has permanence and long-standing tenure. Why do we want to hold on for dear life to the aspects of church life and community that are clearly not working anymore?
>
> It brings me back to my first call and what my head of staff would say, "Anything worth doing well is worth doing poorly." I struggled to figure out what that meant and really railed against it, but now I think I know more what he meant. It's an attitude of "Just try it," "It doesn't have to last forever," "You won't move ahead until you move," and "Why not?" instead of "Why?"

As Gail illustrates, the life of faith faces a unique challenge when it comes to changing our minds. Early faith experiences and learning tend to have deep roots. They become the foundation for adult faith or, if our experience was negative, for a life of no faith at all. And because these beliefs, rooted in revelation, conviction, and authority, are about *God*, they become beyond question and doubt. But that's not the heart of religious or spiritual practice, as Richard Rohr notes in a recent online daily meditation, where he speaks about beginner's mind:

> "Beginner's mind" is actually someone who's *not* in their mind at all! They are people who can immediately experience the naked moment apart from filtering it through any mental categories. Such women and men are capable of simple presence to what is right in front of them without "thinking" about it too much. This must be what Jesus means by little children already being in the kingdom of God (Matthew 18:3–4). They don't think much, they just experience the moment—good and bad. That teaching alone should have told us that Christianity was not supposed to be about believing doctrines and moralities…. Beginner's mind is pure presence to each moment before I label it, critique it, categorize it, exclude it, or judge it up or down. That is a whole new way of thinking and living. It is the only mind that has the power to actually reform religion.[4]

In chapter 10 of the book of Acts, Peter faces a challenge to his beliefs, but then exhibits a presence of mind that helps him see a deeper truth. He falls asleep on a rooftop and dreams of a sheet lowered from heaven filled with forbidden animals and a voice that says, "Get up, Peter; kill and eat." But Peter refuses—it is against his faith. He replies, "By no means, Lord; for I have never eaten anything that is profane or unclean."

Peter's dream occurs three times. Finally he realizes that the dream is not tempting him to do wrong, but showing him what is deeply true—we should not reject what God has accepted. As popular Christian author Hope Egan writes in *Holy Cow! Does God Care about What We Eat?*, until his vision, Peter's understanding was that as a Jew, he was not to associate with non-Jews. This was based on the Jewish interpretation in first-century Israel of the laws of ritual purity—what is clean and unclean—where non-Jews were classified as unclean and to be avoided. Eating with them was discouraged; entering their homes was regarded as contaminating. But

Peter's assumption was in error. There was no biblical basis for the restriction, it was only an interpretation drawn from an agenda of the times. As Peter explains in Acts 10:28, "God has shown me that I should not call any person common or unclean" (ESV). God's love is for all people. God is bigger than Peter thought.

Childlike Faith versus a Child's Faith

Like the story of Peter in Acts, an evolving understanding of God and of the spiritual life gives our faith lives vitality. When we apply beginner's mind to our faith lives, we see that God continues to invite us to learn and grow beyond the faith of our childhood.

I experienced the benefits of rethinking my childhood faith firsthand. At the wise old age of twenty-four, I decided to attend an East Coast seminary that was outside the tradition in which I was raised and educated. In the weeks prior to leaving for seminary, I received several warnings from friends and mentors—"Don't lose your faith." I assured them I would not. I was simply going to seminary to take my boat of faith out of the water and rebuild it. And when I was done, I'd relaunch my bigger and better boat of faith back into the water, ready to start my ministry. How naive! I learned soon enough that my boat of faith never leaves the water. While I was pulling up boards and expanding the hull, I was taking on water and my faith was going under. My friends' worries came true—I did lose my faith. But only to find a reconstituted, more nimble faith that was better able to sail the seas of life. Sometimes we must "lose" our faith in order to more deeply find it.

No Graven Images

It's not just our faith that can get mired in preconceptions and past experience. Children have such a fluid sense of who they are, trying on all kinds of personalities and being whoever their imaginations can create. But it is also in childhood that our self-image is formed by the powerful influences of our parents, family, culture, and experience. As adults, we can become anchored by this self-image, a graven image, which prevents us from growing beyond what was, to what is and can be. As Rabbi Irwin Kula advises us in his book *Yearnings: Embracing the Sacred Messiness of Life,*

> All images, whether societal or personal, become stultifying if we
> don't allow them to change and grow as we do. The second of the
> Ten Commandments urges us not to make a graven image of God.
> Graven images are not only statues; our conception and ideas can
> become just as concrete.[5]

To become like a child, to cultivate beginner's mind, is an invitation
for us to reimagine who we are and set ourselves free from self-images
imposed on us by others. Has our image of ourselves or of others become
an unchanging statue? What would it mean to have beginner's mind, not
only about God and our faith but also about ourselves?

My experience of losing my faith in seminary, only to find it again in the
same place, was also an experience of losing my sense of self, only to find
it more profoundly. My early faith experiences came with certain notions
about God, but they were also filled with powerful notions of who I was.
The notion that I was, at heart, a depraved sinner had been so deeply
ingrained in me that my experiences of God's forgiveness did not touch
it. It was only as I began to open my mind to other ways of seeing myself
that I could finally experience a deeper sense of who I was. Yes, we are
sinners—we do miss the mark—but that is not our truest identity. We are
beloved children of God.

The invitation to become like a child is an invitation to willingly choose to
return to beginner's mind, as inspiring nonfiction author Diane Ackerman
describes in her book *Deep Play*:

> One *chooses* to divest oneself of preconceptions, hand-me-down
> ideas, and shopworn opinions, *chooses* to wipe the mental slate
> clean, *chooses* to be naïve and wholly open to the world, as one
> once was as a child. If cynicism is inevitable as one ages, so is the
> yearning for innocence. To children heaven is being an adult, and
> to adults heaven is being children again.[6]

This does not mean we throw away all that we know. In integral theory,
as described by Ken Wilbur, founder of the Integral Institute, we find
the compelling notion that human and spiritual development incorpo-
rates what has gone before and transforms it into a new, larger whole.[7]
Becoming like a child means we hold on to what we know with an open

hand, not a fist, so we might retain what is life-giving and meaningful, and let go of what no longer serves us or the world. And with that same open hand, we can receive, with curiosity and delight, new wisdom and insight about ourselves, the world, and the mystery we call God.

Practices

A Fist and an Open Hand

Sit comfortably and take a few moments to slow your breath and quiet your mind. When you are ready, make a fist with your dominant hand and for the next minute simply notice what that is like and what images, thoughts, and feelings arise. As you continue to make a fist, let what you are so certain about come to mind. Choose one idea or belief to focus on as you consider:

> How has your mind become like a fist, closed tightly around that idea or belief?

> How has holding that belief, idea, or attitude so tightly served you and others?

Now allow your hand to slowly open, as if your hand has become a cup. What would it mean to hold those particular beliefs or ideas more loosely, to allow other beliefs and ideas to fill the cup of your hand?

> What are you open to learning more about?

> If you experience a lightness or some relief, what might this new freedom signify?

> If you experience fear or anxiety, what is that fear about?

> How might you practice less of a white-knuckle grip on things and more of an open and loose holding of things?

> How might you find a way to practice this in your daily life?

Meditation

This might seem like the simplest of practices, but it is more difficult than it appears because we soon encounter the way our habitual ways of thinking, acting, and feeling are running on automatic pilot. The practice of meditation creates space between these habitual ways of being and opens us to beginner's mind, helping free us to think, feel, and act differently.

Set aside 20 to 30 minutes five out of seven days during the coming week to "simply" meditate. Choose a simple word or phrase as a mantra—for example, *grace*, or *love*, or *Jesus Christ, Son of God, have mercy on me*—or simply concentrate your focus on your breath. When you find your mind wandering, just return to your word, phrase, or breath.

What do you notice when you become this still?

What does your mind do on its own?

Do not judge what your mind does. Just observe it, watch it, and let it go.

Draw What You Feel

Put a large piece of sketching paper or construction paper on a table or desk; gather a set of colored pencils, crayons, or magic markers and place them within easy reach. Take a moment or two to settle in and let go of expectations—what you are about to create has no predetermined way it is supposed to look.

When you're ready, close your eyes, and then reach for a crayon, pencil, or marker—it doesn't matter what color you choose. With your eyes still closed, hold the crayon or marker in the air and make circles or triangles, or any shape you want with your arm, as if you were drawing on the air. Do this as freely as you can, making any kind of movement that you want to.

Once you feel loosened up, with your eyes still closed, start marking on the piece of paper, using any motion or movement you want. Be as free as you can, and when you want to, choose another crayon or marker and make some more marks until you are done.

How does it feel to create without seeing what you're creating?

If you feel a sense of excitement or wonder, what is that about?

If you feel a sense of fear, or perhaps even an inability to move the crayon across the paper, what does that fear stem from?

How might you move past this fear so you can freely move the marker?

When you are done, open your eyes to see what you have created and spend some time reflecting on it.

What's beautiful about it?

What surprises you about it?

How do you feel when you look at it?

7 Let It Be and Let It Go

PRACTICING FORGIVENESS AS A CHOICE AND A GIFT

> Then Peter came and said to him, "Lord, if another member of the church sins against me, how often should I forgive? As many as seven times?" Jesus said to him, "Not seven times, but, I tell you, seventy times seven."
>
> MATTHEW 18:21–22

> The root meaning of the verb "to forgive" is "to let go, to give back, to cease to harbor." Looked at this way, forgiveness is a restful activity. Far more work is required to cling to a judgment than to let go of it.
>
> HUGH PRATHER

One day years ago, Matt, my five-year-old brother, came into the house crying. He ran into his room and as he slammed the door he shouted, "I *hate* Kenny!" The family made an unspoken, collective decision to let him cool down on his own. Thirty minutes later, at the dinner table, he was sullen and quiet. Dad asked what happened.

"Kenny called me a name and then he hit me, and so I hit him back!"

"Well, I'm sure you'll work it out," Dad responded.

"No! I hate Kenny."

My brother stayed quiet throughout dinner and the conversation moved on to my sister's possible choices for a high school homecoming date, Mom's garden, and the difficulty I was having learning a new dive for the swim team.

Suddenly the doorbell rang. Dad pushed back from the table and saw Kenny's nose pressed up against the window on our front door. Dad looked at my brother and said, "It's Kenny." Matt jumped up and shouted, "Kenny!" He ran toward the door with a huge smile on his face. What happened between them was forgotten and forgiven.

I can't tell you how many times that happened!

What Is Forgiveness, Exactly?

This illustration of my brother's easy forgiveness is not unusual among children. Unlike adults, children take life's bumps and bruises in stride. They seem to have a natural ability to move past grievances that only minutes before seemed grave and all-consuming. Whether a wrong has been done to them intentionally—someone threw a snowball at them—or unintentionally—a soccer ball spins off course and bonks them in the back—children are more likely to acknowledge the action, express their feelings (in anger, in tears), accept the apology, and move on. This doesn't mean children don't learn from their experiences. Rather, it means they are less likely than adults to let the facts of reality—that people make mistakes—negatively affect their mental and emotional well-being over the long term. Children choose to go forward, not backward.

We adults, on the other hand, often handle the wrongs that have been done to us—intentionally or unintentionally—differently than children. We're prone to harboring grudges and resentment, replaying offenses in our minds over and over again until what may have been an annoyance festers into rage and hate. We often long for vengeance—the offenders, perceived or real, getting payback for what they have done. As Christian theologian Lewis B. Smedes explains it, what makes forgiveness so difficult, so complex, is that it goes against our human nature of "ledger keeping." Forgiveness, Smedes says, "is outrageous. When we do it we commit an outrage against the strict morality that will not rest with anything short of an even score."[1]

Smedes's observation shows that perhaps we're not clear on what exactly forgiveness is. Many people think forgiveness requires both parties to reach a mutual reconciliation—but forgiveness is granted by the person who has been harmed or offended. It is a conscious decision to move past the hurt. It doesn't require the offender's involvement at all. People also think forgiveness must involve forgetting, condoning, or excusing the harmful actions. This is not the case. Offenses are real; the responsibility for the harmful actions still lies with the offender. But the ones offended, harmed, or hurt genuinely choose, with their hearts, to let go of how they feel about it. They no longer hold it against the other.

The Grace of Forgiveness

While forgiveness is an act performed by the person offended, it involves a gift rooted in grace for the offender. In the Gospel of Matthew Peter asks Jesus how many times he should forgive those who sin against him. Peter wonders if it could be as many as seven times. Jesus says to him, "Not seven times, but, I tell you, seventy times seven" (18:21–22).

Jesus then tells a parable. A king wants to settle accounts with his slaves. One slave owes ten thousand talents. A talent was a measurement for gold or silver. One talent was equivalent to a peasant's lifetime of earnings. What this slave owes is almost unimaginable to Jesus's hearers. The slave begs for patience; he will repay the debt. Out of pity, the king releases him and forgives the debt.

The slave comes upon one of his fellow slaves who owes him a hundred denarii—a drop in the bucket compared to his own ocean of debt. He seizes his fellow slave by the throat and says, "Pay me what you owe." His fellow slave pleads for patience; he will repay the debt. The slave who is owed the pittance has the other slave thrown in jail.

The king hears about this incident and says to the slave whose debt he forgave, "You wicked slave! I forgave you all that debt because you pleaded with me. Should you not have had mercy on your fellow slave, as I had mercy on you?" (See Matthew 18:23–35.)

As this parable shows, forgiveness gives offenders more than they deserve. That's why the loan imagery in this parable of Jesus is so powerful. No one forgives a monetary debt like that! It shows that the wrongs we do to one another are to be dealt with on a different level. It's not a business ledger, where the goal is equal balance, but a ledger of grace, a grace that (for)gives.

When this grace finds you, touches you, convinces you—when it works its way underneath your carefully constructed defenses—it is liberating. The weight of guilt we carry for our wrongful actions is not fully understood until forgiveness lifts it and the freedom of grace *received* is experienced. How burdened we were!

The same is true for the person who forgives. The burden of a grudge, resentment, or bitterness is not fully understood until the act of forgiving another lifts it and the freedom of grace *given* is experienced. How weighed down we are with being unforgiving! In *God's Tender Mercy: Reflections on Forgiveness*, Benedictine nun and author Joan Chittister candidly described the effects of refusing to grant forgiveness by saying, "What I refuse to forgive continues to harm me. It consumes my heart, poisons my mind, drains my energies, and cements my soul."[2] When you truly forgive from the heart, as Jesus describes forgiveness, you know it by the liberation of your own soul. The forgiveness is not simply spoken, not grudgingly offered; it is felt and real.

Forgiveness: A Way of Living

Peter's guess on the appropriate number of times he should forgive someone—seven—belies an underlying assumption about humanity that Jesus does not share. Peter assumes there is a limit, that others should, after a certain amount of time, get it right. Jesus assumes there is no limit, not only in our capacity for forgiveness, but also in our need for forgiveness. Forgiveness is the grease on our wheels, the oil in our engine, the currency in the human economy. Because we are imperfect human beings, we will always let each other down and do things that hurt one another. And as we become more self-aware and wiser—as we see and understand the many and subtle ways we give in to our egos and frailties, and don't recognize what we're doing to ourselves or others—we will take less offense at the things others do that previously we would have taken personally. But even here, in this place of wisdom, the need for forgiveness is present, as Jesus demonstrates so powerfully when he says of those who had just crucified him, "Father, forgive them, for they do not know what they are doing" (Luke 23:34). The health and vitality of our relationships depend on forgiveness being offered and received.

A pastor friend and mentor of mine filed for divorce after twenty-five years of marriage. His wife was shocked and greatly hurt, their children were quite upset with him, and the church he had served with a great deal of energy and time for over ten years decided it was time to move in a new direction. Not long afterward my friend married again, exacerbating the suspicions already running rampant in the community. His ex-wife struggled to find work; she was embarrassed to be seen at church, the supermarket, or at her children's sporting events. She grappled with self-recrimination, doubt, and shame. A fairly calm woman by nature, she found herself seething with anger, resentment, and bitterness toward her ex-husband. She was going through hell because of him, and because of their children, the house, and alimony, she had to maintain a relationship with him. She hated it.

I visited my pastor friend about five years later. He and his new wife were doing well. When I asked about his children, he went into great detail about a cruise they all took together and how good it was to see them and their mother. I said, "Excuse me?" He said, "Tim, I know it's hard to believe myself, but she has forgiven me. She really has. We probably have a better relationship now than we ever had when we were married. She has really worked hard on herself and I'm very proud and grateful we can be together with our children and really care for each other."

Shortly after that visit, I returned to the town where we had worked together to officiate at the marriage of one of the teenagers who had been in the youth group, and I visited my friend's ex-wife. We had lunch together at a downtown restaurant and I asked her to tell me about the change that happened in her. She said, "The divorce really threw me for a loop, and it was so painful, but it caused me to turn and face some of my own issues. With a counselor's help, I began to see that I had minimized the signs that our relationship was eroding, and I realized how I had stopped growing myself. The anger and bitterness I held toward him was akin to the anger and bitterness I had for myself, and I began to see how it was eating me alive. I was becoming an angry, bitter, diminished woman.

"But it slowly dawned on me that I had choices about the way I would see myself and the way I would see him. I am so grateful that I got to the place where I could really forgive myself and forgive him. I saw what the anger and bitterness were doing to me and I didn't want to live that way or be that way. He's still in many ways the same man he was, and so we still butt heads—actually, a little bit more than we did before because I am now willing to put my two cents in much more than before—so I still need to forgive him and myself. But I wouldn't trade it for anything now. I've found myself. The relationship with our children has flourished, and there is genuine love and care for each other. Being able to forgive myself and him has changed everything, and we are all better for it."

Forgiveness experienced leads to forgiveness extended. Or, to put it another way, there is an economy of forgiveness. It is not earned, but there is a flow to it. It cannot be fully received until it's fully offered; fully offering it allows it to be fully received; and fully receiving it flows out into fully offering it to others. As the Lord's Prayer puts it, "Forgive us our debts, as we forgive our debtors." In this sense, giving and receiving forgiveness are hand in glove—inseparable. And because they are inseparable, being unforgiving means there is a price we will pay.

The Price of Seeking Payment

At the end of Jesus's parable about forgiveness, we read that the king "handed [the unforgiving slave] over to be tortured until he should pay his entire debt." Then Jesus says, "So my heavenly Father will also do to every one of you, if you do not forgive your brother or sister from your heart" (Matthew 18:34–35).

The king's response to the wicked slave in Jesus's parable seems to portray God as harsh and tormenting. But the phrase *handed him over* is a way of indicating that when we are unforgiving of others, we are the ones who become imprisoned and pay the price. When we do not forgive, we remain trapped in our own bitterness, resentment, and anger, which eat at us from the inside.

Neil Rosenthal, a syndicated relationship-advice columnist and a therapist, had this to say to an ex-husband about his unwillingness to forgive:

> Your pain and anger are likely not hurting your ex-wife, but they
> are clearly hurting you. It's your peace of mind that's destroyed,
> it's your body that is tightening up, it's your mind that is tortured

by what happened—because resentment, hurt and anger all bind us to other people just as effectively as love does, but in a negative way.[3]

If we do not forgive those who have hurt us, we nurse grievances, plan revenge, ignore, criticize, or ostracize others—or ourselves. If we do not forgive, we pray that God will show the other person he is wrong and teach him a lesson, and we subtly rejoice when something in his life goes awry. Like the servant in the parable, in subtle or not-so-subtle ways, we demand that others pay. When we do this, we are choosing to be tied to people negatively. However, if we choose to forgive, we tie ourselves to others in love, and love is freeing. Which one will we choose?

That question is difficult to stomach, for it often feels as if we cannot forgive; we can't let it go. But as the story of my brother and his friend Kenny shows, when we embrace childlike forgiveness, we learn to forgive not just once, but many times. Forgiveness is an ongoing process, not a once-and-for-all event. The more we practice forgiveness, the better able we are to let offenses go. They fall away because we are no longer holding on to them and rehashing them over and over in our minds.

Our Unvoiced Prayers

Whether we know it or not, our lives are prayers. Our intentions toward others, whether conscious or unconscious, play out as prayers. We wish others wholeness or harm, freedom or constraint, joy or suffering, blessing or curse.

Mark Twain captured this truth in his work "The War Prayer." During a time of war, national fervor swelled as the people gathered at the church to pray for God's blessings on the young soldiers heading off to war. The pastor, filled with passion, offered a long prayer asking God to help them crush the foe and grant their country glory. An aged stranger walked up the aisle and stood silently by the pastor until he finished. Startled, the pastor let the stranger speak. He said, "I come from the Throne—bearing a message from Almighty God!" The stranger said that God had heard their prayer and would answer it, if they truly understood that their prayer was two—the one voiced, and the one not voiced. He then prayed the unvoiced prayer:

Lord our Father, our young patriots, idols of our hearts, go forth into battle—be Thou near them! With them—in spirit—we also go forth from the sweet peace of our beloved firesides to smite the foe. O Lord our God, help us tear their soldiers to bloody shreds with our shells; help us to cover their smiling fields with the pale forms of their patriot dead; help us to drown the thunder of the guns with the shrieks of their wounded, writhing in pain; help us to lay waste their humble homes with a hurricane of fire; help us to wring the hearts of their unoffending widows with unavailing grief; help us to turn them out roofless with their little children to wander unfriended in the wastes of their desolated land in rags and hunger and thirst, sports of the sun flames in summer and the icy winds of winter, broken in spirit, worn with travail, imploring Thee for the refuge of the grave and denied it. For our sakes who adore Thee, Lord, blast their hopes, blight their lives, protract their bitter pilgrimage, make heavy their steps, water their way with their tears, stain the white snow with the blood of their wounded feet! We ask it, in the spirit of love, of Him Who is the Source of Love, and Who is the ever-faithful refuge and friend of all that are sore beset and seek His aid with humble and contrite hearts. Amen.[4]

"The War Prayer" story ends with these words: "It was believed afterward that the man was a lunatic, because there was no sense in what he said." When "The War Prayer" was refused by his publisher, Mark Twain asked that it not be published until after his death because, as he said, "I have told the whole truth in it, and only dead men can tell the truth in this world." Twain died in 1910 and it was not published until after World War I, in 1923.

Breaking the Cycle One Heart at a Time

Forgiveness from the heart is exemplified by the aged stranger in "The War Prayer." Forgiveness is viewed as lunacy, until we see what the flip side of refusing to forgive is all about and recognize a far greater lunacy. Refusing to forgive means we perpetuate ad infinitum the anger, bitterness, and revenge that lives in our hearts, and it becomes an unending cycle of emotional, mental, spiritual, and physical violence in the world. The smaller this world gets, the greater the need for forgiveness.

I am now divorced, but in the early years of my marriage, my wife and I walked into a jewelry shop to get her ring cleaned. We soon found ourselves in a conversation with the shop owner. He was upset about the situation in the Middle East. Then he said, "We should gather up all the Palestinian and Iraqi terrorists, shoot them all without question, and then sit the rest of them down and say, 'Look, this is what we will do, so just stop the killing.'"

I could have kept my mouth shut, but that would have shown my tacit endorsement of the jeweler's stated "eye for an eye" philosophy. But I was aware that *how* I talked with the jeweler was just as important as *what* I said. I told him I could understand his point of view all too well. I commented on my own impulse to lash out, punish, and demean, but I didn't think it seemed to work very well because it only resulted in more of the same. I said, "Your proposal simply perpetuates the killing, because the very attitude *you* have will now be engendered in the *Muslims*, who will then turn around and attempt to do the very thing you've just done."

"But how does it stop, then?" he asked.

I said, "It stops with you and me. One person at a time. We must forgive."

No Easy Path to Forgiveness

As all of us know, forgiveness is not easy and it seems almost impossible to comprehend when people extend forgiveness in the cases of monumental tragedies, vicious attacks, and gruesome acts of violence. Yet time and again we learn of such miracles. When we wonder about the source of such forgiveness, we need only look to the Christian tradition for examples and support.

> A woman caught committing adultery was brought to Jesus, and the scribes and Pharisees said to him, "In the Law, Moses commanded us to stone such women. Now what do you say?"
>
> Jesus said, "Let anyone among you who is without sin be the first to throw a stone at her." One by one the accusers left.
>
> Jesus said to the woman, "Woman, where are they? Has no one condemned you?"
>
> She said, "No one, sir."
>
> Jesus then said, "Neither do I condemn you." (See John 8:1–11.)

When the prodigal son, after squandering his share of the inheritance, returns home, his father runs out to greet him with kisses, adorns him with the best robe and a ring, sandals for his feet, and throws a feast in celebration.

On the cross Jesus prays, "Father, forgive them; they don't know what they are doing."

We can find inspiration in our own day as well. On September 12, 2001, one day after the twin towers of the World Trade Center in New York were destroyed by terrorists, the *San Francisco Chronicle* published a letter to the editor from Lou Bordisso, a priest from the city of Walnut Creek. He wrote,

> I searched in vain in the special *Chronicle* Sept. 11 section for the names of the terrorists on the list of those to be remembered and prayed for. It is easy and comfortable for our nation to remember our hero firefighters, those who perished in the twin towers, the Pentagon and in Pennsylvania, but somehow we are unable to keep close to our hearts the hijackers and their loved ones as well. Has our nation forgotten the notion to love our enemies and to pray for those who persecute us? Who is it that has uttered, "Forgive them, Abba, for they know not what they do?" If we are a Christian nation, rooted in Judeo-Christian values, then forgiveness is really not an option. It's a calling. It's what love does. If Christ lives in us, forgiveness lives in us. And we forget it at our peril, and the world's peril.

When we are wronged, anger and rage naturally surface. We have to wrestle with that rage before it can be transformed into forgiveness. Michael Sells, a professor of world religions, addressing a packed house at the University of North Carolina, spoke of the rage we felt when loved ones and innocents were harmed on September 11. He suggested that outrage is an essential component of love. But that rage must not move to vengeance, he said; otherwise, the cycle of violence is perpetuated. Rather, we must turn the rage into light, like a laser beam, to work for good. He mentioned the Texas couple who turned their rage at the abduction and death of their daughter into the Amber Alert program, designed to save hundreds, if not thousands, of children from a similar fate.

Another example of a person wrestling with rage is Bud Welch. In 1995, Welch's daughter, Julie, died in the bombing of the Alfred P. Murrah Federal Building in Oklahoma City. Prior to the 2001 execution of Timothy McVeigh, the man partially responsible for that bombing, Welch said,

> The first month after the bombing, I didn't want Tim McVeigh or Terry Nichols to even have trials. I simply wanted them fried. And then I came to realize that the reason Julie and 167 others were dead is because of vengeance and rage. And when we take him out of his cage to kill him, it's going to be the same thing. We will keep the circle going. Number 169 dead is not going to help the family members of the first 168.[5]

In the years since his daughter's death, Welch has become a prominent opponent of the death penalty, often reflecting on his deceased daughter's words that executions were only "teaching children to hate."

We are called on to forgive, and that is extremely difficult. That does not mean we forget what wrongdoers have done to us. But it does mean we turn our rage into light, to build a better world.

And then, when we have forgiven, we often find an unexpected and grace-filled outcome. We find that we *have* forgotten in a sense—we've let it go. When we keep turning the offense over and over in our mind and heart—rehashing the bitterness, resentment, grudges, and desire for revenge—we keep the memory of the hurt alive. But when we offer forgiveness, we let it go in such a way that it's emotional, energetic charge dissipates. We no longer obsess, dwell on, or return to it, and we discover that it vanishes from our mind. I want to be clear here. We are not the ones who do the forgetting; it's not an intentional act on our part. But the dynamics of genuine forgiveness, the letting go of the emotional charge, results in a kind of forgetfulness. It subsides because it is no longer being fed by our thoughts, emotions, and energy.

A wonderful Zen koan points to forgetfulness that comes as gift, as grace. Two monks were walking home after a rainstorm when they came upon a beautiful princess stranded by a swollen stream. She feared crossing and asked if the monks might carry her across the stream. The first monk hesitated but the second monk picked her up and carried her across the stream. The princess offered her thanks and the monks resumed their journey home in silence. Finally, the first monk could no longer stay silent. "How could you have done that?" he said. "You know we are not to touch or hold a woman, especially one as beautiful as that princess!"

The monk who had carried the princess said, "I put her down a long time ago. You are the one who is continuing to hold on to her."[6]

When we have offered genuine forgiveness, we find that we forget—we let go—but it is not of our own doing. It is a gift of grace.

Forgiving as a Way to Restore Wholeness

As Lewis B. Smedes points out, forgiveness is not something offered because we will get something in return. The prefix *for* indicates "to the uttermost or extremely," and *give* means "to present voluntarily without expecting compensation." But the act of forgiveness, paradoxically, offers us the interior freedom to move toward wholeness. Forgiveness from the heart is a gift to others and to ourselves.

Children have the ability to live their lives this way, forgiving without feeling a need to get anything in return. Gerald May tells this story about his young son, Paul.

> We used to live next door to a grouchy old man. He put up a chain-link fence when our children began to play in the backyard. We tried to make friends with him, but he would have none of it. He threatened to kill my son Paul's kitten after it strayed into his rosebushes. "I see that cat on my land again, I'll poison it," he said. Paul, who was four at the time, became obsessed with keeping the kitten inside. He'd wake up screaming at night. A few days later the kitten was dead. We saw it die and we were sure it had been poisoned. While the rest of the family was grieving and making up fantasies about what we could do for revenge, Paul grew very quiet. Finally he had something to say about our neighbor. "He must be very lonely. Maybe we should give him a birthday party or something."[7]

Forgiveness may be one of the most difficult ways for us to become like children. As adults, we seem to maintain a ledger of misdeeds and hold tightly to old wrongs, parceling out love or kindness only to the deserving.

But who among us is deserving? Who among us is without moments of mistake and misdirection? We must choose forgiveness, not just once, or only seven times, but seventy times seven. The late Methodist minister Hugh Prather summed up this concept concisely in *Morning Notes: 365 Meditations to Wake You Up*: "Forgive, but do not wonder how you must act. Forgive, but do not try to convince another to forgive. Forgive, but do not hold yourself superior that you have done so. Simply forgive."[8]

Practices

What Am I Holding on To?

After a few minutes of centering and grounding, bring to your awareness the grudges you are holding on to, the people you have not forgiven. This may be difficult, but allow yourself to feel what you really feel, and bring to mind the wrongs you feel have been done to you.

Now, consider what effects holding on to these grudges and the feelings associated with them are having on you. What attitudes and behaviors result? Are you happy with them?

Now ask yourself whether you are expecting something from these people first in order to forgive them or whether anything will enable you to forgive them. Does the forgiveness depend on them or on you?

What are you willing to let go of?

What are you not willing to let go of?

The Log in Our Own Eye

In the Gospel of Luke, Jesus says to first take the log out of our own eye and then we will see clearly enough to help another take the splinter out of her eye. This parable helps us to recognize that often the very thing we do not forgive in another is a transgression we ourselves have committed. After getting into a contemplative place, ask yourself in what ways you have not forgiven yourself.

What are you still holding against yourself?

Where did those expectations and demands come from?

Are you willing to forgive yourself?

If not, what prevents you from doing so?

Just as forgiving others can often be a long process, so too is it with forgiving ourselves. This prayer practice can also evoke difficult and tender emotions, so please be as patient and kind with yourself as possible, as you move toward forgiving yourself, rooted in God's forgiveness.

8 Fully Embodied, Fully Inspirited

Recognizing and Reading Your Body as a Source of Wisdom

David danced before the Lord with all his might.

2 SAMUEL 6:14

I appeal to you therefore, brothers and sisters,
by the mercies of God, to present your bodies
as a living sacrifice, holy and acceptable to
God, which is your spiritual worship.

ROMANS 12:1–2

I feel good!

JAMES BROWN

Several years ago, we gathered for Thanksgiving at my cousin's house. There was plenty of food to eat and stories to tell, but most of the attention was paid to my cousin's fourteen-month-old son. After dinner he was plopped on top of the table in front of his cooing grandmother and great-aunts, and a pumpkin pie with vanilla ice cream was presented to him. It was to be his first bite of this holiday treat. I wish we had taken a video! The taste, texture, and temperatures of cold ice cream and warm pumpkin pie hit his sensory system like lightning. Delight bolted through the entire length of his body in a series of flailing arms, snapping legs, and whole-body gyrations, not to mention eyebrows that arched off his face. We laughed until tears ran down our faces as we watched what I would call *incarnation*. Taste was embodied!

Beginning with the Body

The body is the beginning of wisdom. From our very first breath, our mind and heart develop through our body. We learn hunger, thirst, temperature, pleasure, pain, discomfort, love, and disapproval with the body, and through it we discover the world and how it works. From infancy into our childhood years, we continue to channel our emotions through our body without inhibition. Think about a child freely dancing because he is happy or moved by music in the middle of the grocery store, or a child throwing her arms wide and running to a loving parent, fully open to welcome and receive the parent's adoration. This is what makes children so easy to read.

As adults, we lose this body-mind connection. Considering ourselves and our emotions intellectually takes precedence over what we might be saying with our bodies. This is due, in part, to the effect Greek dualism has had on Western culture and its religious and spiritual traditions, elevating spirit above matter. Our culture makes us suspicious of the body. As Rabbi Bradley Shavit Artson explains in *God of Becoming and Relationships: The Dynamic Nature of Process Theology*, we have the Greek philosopher Plato to thank for this:

> It was Plato who taught us that the ideal cannot be physical. A physical chair, while related to all other chairs on some level, is always faulty—it gets scratched, it breaks, it doesn't balance perfectly. But the concept of the chair, the idea of the chair—that's where chair perfection is to be found. Plato believed in that ideal, that somehow if one could distill the essence of something beyond its mere physicality, we would encounter its perfect exemplar.... From this viewpoint, the realm of spirit is actually more real, more worthy, than its imperfect, physical shadow.[1]

Christianity and other religious traditions affected by this dualism have tended to denigrate if not demonize the body and its accompanying desires as something to overcome and rise above. Take, for example, Thomas à Kempis's *Imitation of Christ*. In it we read,

> Sometimes you must use violence and resist your sensual appetite bravely. You must pay no attention to what the flesh does or does not desire, taking pains that it be subjected, even by force, to the spirit. And it should be chastised and forced to remain in subjection until it is prepared for anything and is taught to be satisfied with little.[2]

Even our praying is mostly with our head. When we pray, we think, and if feelings arise in our prayers, we tend to think about those feelings instead of experiencing them in our bodies. The result? We live in our heads and have lost the ability to read our bodies for the wisdom they impart to us, so much so that we live as if we were disembodied.

To become like children is an invitation for us to get back into our bodies and see them as sources of wisdom and truth.

Listening to and with the Body

Our bodies are a source of wisdom, for tapping into the Spirit's presence. They are a catalyst for transforming attitude, feeling, and mood. For example, "a pit in my stomach" can simply be passed off as something I ate. But by paying closer attention to my body, I may realize I am tense about an upcoming meeting. This knowledge allows me to explore what the tension is about and to work through it.

Throughout history there are many examples of prayers and practices that engage the body, use the body, and invite the body's wisdom. The Jesus Prayer, dating back to the sixth century, combines the natural rhythm of our breath with the words "Jesus Christ, Son of God [breathe in], have mercy on me, a sinner [breathe out]." The exact words are not as important as the intent of the prayer—to open our heart, mind, soul, and body to God's presence, and to keep returning to the breath and the words when our mind wanders. By tying the words and the breath together, we soon realize that instead of owning and controlling our breath, we are breathed, and so too are we breathed by God. With the prayer so closely attuned to our breath, a deep sigh during a tense meeting at work or in an important conversation with a loved one will reveal that we are naturally praying.

The Prayer of the Heart, building on the Jesus Prayer, calls for bowing the head to look in the direction of the heart, and invites us to listen for the heart's longings and wisdom. The heart—a metaphor for the integration of mind, will, emotion, desire, and the presence of God—has a language of its own, with a different tenor and tone than raw desire or ego-centered wishes and wants. Listening to the heart and body is a way of discerning our deeper, truer longings.

The prayer known as Body Scan, or Body Prayer, prompts us to slowly scan the various parts of our body, noticing the sensations in the body and reflecting on the meaning of those sensations. This prayer is associated with fourteenth-century medieval mystic Julian of Norwich, who in her *Showings* (or *Revelations*) heralded the body-mind-spirit connection and its relationship to God:

> For he does not despise what he has made, nor does he disdain to serve us in the simplest natural functions of our body, for love of the soul which he created in his own likeness.
>
> For as the body is clad in the cloth, and the flesh in the skin, and the bones in the flesh, and the heart in the trunk, so are we, soul and body, clad and enclosed in the goodness of God.[3]

Julian knew that furrowed eyebrows, a tight stomach, tension in our shoulders, and shallow breathing communicate something about what is going on inside us—worry, anxiety, fear, anger. When we feel love, gratitude, or trust, those realities will show up in our bodies, too, such as with deep breathing and relaxed muscles. The state of our soul is expressed in our bodies.

Leading with the Body

But it is not just paying attention to our bodies that helps us become childlike and integrate mind, body, and spirit. What our bodies *do* also has a powerful impact on moods, attitudes, and feelings.

The impulse of children to get rambunctious, go play in the yard, or do flips off the side of the couch reveals the power of our bodies to affect our spirit and soul. How many of us, finding ourselves spiritually lethargic, down, or apathetic, try to think or pray our way into a better mood, with little result? But often, engaging our bodies directly and intentionally—by walking, hiking, running, biking, dancing, singing, playing music, drumming, doing yoga or tai chi—can radically transform our moods and attitudes.

Take the simple smile. In *Stress Free for Good*, Dr. Frederic Luskin and Dr. Kenneth R. Pelletier draw a connection between the physical action of smiling and the resulting feeling of happiness. They point to research by Dr. Paul Ekman, at the University of California School of Medicine in San Francisco, who found that smiling stimulates the body's production of endorphins, the naturally occurring opiates that relieve pain and create a sense of pleasure, peace, and well-being. In effect, Ekman's work gives some credence to the adage "Fake it 'til you make it." Luskin and Pelletier conclude,

> Try a smile right now. Think of the love you offer, and smile. Hold that smile for about ten seconds. Every person that we've asked to do this has reported feeling better. In other words, not only do you smile when you feel happy, but you feel happy when you smile! Apparently you can't have one without the other. So if you want to experience a moment of happiness, smile.... A moment of good feeling will follow.[4]

A student in the diploma program in the Art of Spiritual Direction at San Francisco Theological Seminary was meeting with me for spiritual direction when she told me she had started a new spiritual practice that was becoming transformative for her. She began each day by lying prostrate on the floor as she prayed. The position of her body helped her move into the desired intention and internal posture for the kind of prayer she needed at that time in her life, a way to surrender to all that God was doing in her life. She was amazed and grateful that her body led her soul into a powerful way of praying, a way of being.

The Body: The Antenna for the Heart and Mind

Just as learning to read our bodies helps us better understand ourselves, the practice can also help us more deeply engage with others. By becoming sensitive to our own feelings, sensations, and energy surfacing from within, we also become more sensitive to the energy emitted by others. We become like an antenna intercepting radio waves and, with the receiver of our heart and mind, convert the signals into information.

As a spiritual director, I have been in conversations with others when I suddenly sense myself feeling angry or tired. These feelings catch me by surprise because I have no reason to feel like this. But on a closer read of my body, I notice that they're not coming from me—these are feelings I am receiving from the other person. (Psychotherapists call this *counter-transference*.) Once I know this, I can channel our conversation to address these feelings, if the other person is willing to do so. This skill—reading the energy and body language of others, and distinguishing it from our own—is one of the most important skills for counselors and spiritual directors.

I had a recent phone conversation with a friend and former colleague, David Glick, a therapist in Berkeley, California, and a staff member at the Interfaith Counseling Center in San Anselmo, California. He talked about his own experience as a therapist:

> A client will often unconsciously act in a particular way to evoke a feeling in me as the therapist so I might feel what they are feeling inside. For example, let's say a client grew up with a hypercritical father and as a consequence felt diminished and inadequate in his father's presence. This client will act and speak to me in a dismissive way to the point where I begin to feel inadequate as a therapist. My own visceral feelings become clues to what my client felt in his childhood and continues to feel as an adult.

Mind, Body, and Spirit

How can we become more embodied like a child? What might help us pay attention, notice, and employ our bodies as sources of our own wisdom and receptors of God's wisdom and grace? The following words from dancer Megan MacArthur point us in a good direction:

> I dance to open, I dance to connect, I dance to heal and unwind the held patterns and stagnation, I dance to celebrate the unlimited

potential of my body, to mend, to strengthen, condition, lubricate, form and reform, and allow my body to discover and celebrate its original state, its birthright—pleasure.[5]

There is something that happens when we move into the body and allow it to move us, physically, emotionally, and spiritually. As the godfather of soul, James Brown, sang, "I feel good!"

From our twenty-first-century perspective, we can easily castigate the practices of ancient people—their embodied dances, rituals, ceremonies, and festivals—as primitive. But ancient cultures intuited that humans thrive when they integrate body, mind, and soul. Engaging the body, as well as the mind and spirit, is essential to our wholeness.

We get glimpses of this integration, of embodied spiritual living, in the Hebrew and Christian Scriptures. A scene described in 2 Samuel is moving, powerful, and erotic. King David dances nearly naked with all his might before the Lord, in gratitude for God's grace, guidance, and providence. His spontaneous display is just one of the many ways of expressing what it means to "love God with all your heart, mind, soul, and strength." David is embodied; David is like a child.

The Apostle Paul describes the body as a living sacrifice, integral to wholeness and worship. By this he means that we are to use our bodies to fulfill the beauty and purpose of God's creation. As Paul says,

> Do you not know that your body is a temple of the Holy Spirit within you, which you have from God, and that you are not your own? For you were bought with a price; therefore glorify God in your body. (1 Corinthians 6:19–20)

Jesus's ministry and his focus on the kingdom of God encompass the healing of mind, spirit, and body. He senses healing energy leaving his body when a chronically ill woman touches his cloak. He touches the lepers and the lame, not only restoring them to their communities but also restoring their dignity. Perhaps the most important affirmation of the body in the Christian tradition is the idea of incarnation and resurrection. The incarnation points to the Divine living undividedly with humanity, and the resurrection celebrates an embodied eternity. Both are about being embodied!

What We Know through Our Bodies

Our embodied experiences give us the ability to recognize and experience spiritual truths. We would not know what Jesus meant when he said to the woman at the well that the cup he gave her would quench her thirst if we did not know what it was like to have our physical thirst quenched. We might not trust our bodily intuition that something isn't quite right if we had not had the experience of something smelling fishy, rotten. We might not recognize God's goodness to us if we did not have the very bodily experience of tasting delicious and healthy food and delighting in its pleasure and its goodness. When we take greater notice of our bodies, what they are saying to us, and how our emotional, mental, and spiritual health is affected by our bodies, we will find ourselves moving toward wholeness, and our spiritual lives will not be separate from our bodily existence. Salvation is here and now, not just at the end of life. The Spirit is incarnate in our whole lives—body, mind, and spirit.

Practices

Praying with Postures

There are many ways to pray with postures. Begin by taking a few minutes to quiet your mind and body, and invite Spirit's presence to be with you. When you are in a centered place, get in touch with a mood or a feeling you are experiencing, and find a body posture that expresses that mood or feeling. Hold the posture for several minutes and pray the prayers the posture evokes in you. You might find the posture releases other feelings, helping you get in touch with what's going on deep within you. If other feelings or desires arise, find a different posture to express these new feelings and desires.

A variation for praying with postures is to go through a series of postures, and pay attention to the posture that has the most energy, emotion, or impact on you. Take a few minutes after praying with the postures to reflect on your prayer experience and what it might mean for you and your life.

Here is a brief series of postures for exploring praying with your body:

First, stand up straight with your feet hip-distance apart. Place your hands over your heart and close your eyes. Inhale deeply, and let your exhale sigh out of you. Repeat this several times, letting your breath deepen each time. Now take notice: What kind of prayer arises from your body? Give yourself a few minutes to let the prayer unfold.

Then, when you are ready, stand with your feet a little wider apart. Put one hand on your hip, and thrust the other hand, clenched into a fist, into the air and shake it at the sky. Notice what kind of prayer now emerges from your body. Let yourself pray this way for a few minutes.

Finally, when you are ready, spread your arms out wide with your palms up. Let your head fall back as you look upward. What kind of prayer arises now? Which posture unlocked unexpected emotions or surprising prayers? Which posture felt the most natural?

Body Scan

Take a few moments to sit in a comfortable position, or lie on your back on the floor or on a bed. Let yourself breathe naturally and become aware of your breath, and open yourself to the Spirit's presence. Beginning with your toes and feet, simply become aware of the feelings or sensations you notice there. Sometimes there will be little or no sensation at all, or small aches and pains, or a sense of relaxation and ease. Do not judge any of these sensations or lack thereof: Simply notice and pay attention. It can be helpful to "send your breath" to the area of your body to which you are paying attention, as a way of focusing and relaxing. Slowly work your way through your entire body, from toes and feet to ankles, calves, knees, thighs, hamstrings, and so on, until you have listened to your entire body. Take a few minutes to wonder about the various sensations that seemed to have the most energy. What do these feelings suggest to you about your life? What wisdom might they contain?

9 Laughter and a Sense of Humor

GRACE'S DAILY DIETARY REQUIREMENT

You don't stop laughing because you grow old,
you grow old because you stop laughing.

MICHAEL PRITCHARD

Our capacity to love God, ourselves, people, and
all of life grows with our capacity to laugh. We
are ridiculous, and not to laugh at our religions,
our worldviews, and our philosophies (that is,
ourselves) would be a false witness.... This ability
to laugh in the midst of our imperfections in
the presence of God is what we call grace.

SAMIR SELMANOVIC

The monthly meeting of the board of elders at the church was already a bit tense. The financial report had revealed a drop in revenue for the sixth straight month. Then the moderator turned to the next item for discussion: ordination of gays and lesbians. One longtime elder, John, began to talk and soon his voice grew louder and louder until he said, "And if this church chooses to go this way, I will take my family and my money and go elsewhere!" He slammed his hand on the table to make his point. The room fell silent, until two-year-old Maggie, sitting on her mother Lisa's lap, slapped her hand on the table too. Surprised, everyone looked at Maggie. Realizing she had everyone's attention, Maggie slapped her hand on the table again and started laughing. The board of elders erupted in laughter, slapping their hands on the table with her. Even good old John began to laugh, and he slapped his hand on the table quite differently than he had a few moments before. Maggie's comic imitation of John's actions, and her infectious laughter, prompted the board of elders, including John, to release their tension and become more vulnerable about their real feelings, not only about this particular issue but also about their fears of a rapidly changing culture and the difficult process of rethinking what they believed and felt. The discussion became richer.

Laughter: Healthy or Harmful?

It has been said that children laugh up to four hundred times a day and adults only fifteen. While these exact numbers are unproven, it only takes a visit to a playground to know that children win in a landslide over adults when it comes to expressing their feelings and moods through laughter.

Why is that? As adults, we take ourselves so seriously. We're weighted down by self-image, self-importance, self-doubt. We drive our lives on absolutes—if I don't look perfect I'll be the laughing stock of the event; if I don't give a perfect presentation, I'll have no respect from my peers—that leave little room for our perfectly natural human shortcomings. On the road to maturity, our ability to laugh gets crushed beneath the pounds of pressure we put on ourselves to achieve perfect composure.

If we see laughter as a threat to our equanimity, that is nothing new. Laughter has a long history of being seen as potentially dangerous. Plato, whom the *Stanford Encyclopedia of Philosophy* deemed laughter's most influential critic, viewed laughter as the antithesis of rational self-control. He proposed regulating it, fearing that, if left unchecked, laughter could undermine the social order. His thinking, along with that of other critical philosophers, influenced the early Christian church, which advocated joy but saw laughter as undignified or connected to idleness, irresponsibility, lust, or anger.[1] The Rule of St. Benedict, for example, which was written in the sixth century but is the leading guide for Western Christian communal monastic living today, advises:

The tenth degree of humility
is that he be not ready and quick to laugh,
for it is written,
"The fool lifts up his voice in laughter." (Ecclesiastes 21:23)

What the early church leaders may not have known, though, is how good laughing is for us. In "Lighten Up and Laugh," a column in *Psychology Today*, clinical psychologist Dr. Russell Grieger outlines the primary health benefits that laughter, a physiological response, has on our physical and mental well-being. It reduces stress, eases anxiety, helps us bond with people, boosts the immune system, lowers blood pressure, relaxes muscles, and increases tolerance to pain. And, last but not least, it brings us pleasure.[2]

Laughing at Ourselves

Laughter enlivens us. In college I was part of a fellowship of Christian athletes called Godsquad. We met on Wednesday nights for fellowship and on Sundays we often sang—yes, sang—in churches all over Indiana and Ohio. Many of us were not officially athletes and many of us could not sing a lick. It didn't matter.

One spring day Godsquad's intramural softball team faced off against Dativus, the rowdiest social club on campus. I don't want to pigeonhole anyone, but for the most part Dativus members saw us as goody-two-shoes. You could see them rubbing their hands together, anticipating a slaughter of biblical proportions on the softball field.

Just before the game was to begin, one of our members, nicknamed Cricket, gathered us together on the pitcher's mound for prayer. As we knelt down, Dativus responded with smirks: "Religious bigots." Cricket began to pray loudly with his best imitation of a camp-meeting evangelist. He prayed for a good game, for no injuries, for good sportsmanship, and "this opportunity for fellowship with our brothers in Dativus." And then he said, "But Lord, most of all, today we pray," and he paused for emphasis, "that we kick their #@%$*& asses!" We erupted in laughter, and Dativus did, too. Cricket's prayer invited all of us to laugh at ourselves, to see how seriously we had taken our respective perspectives on life, and how we had misjudged each other. I don't remember who won the game, but it didn't matter.

Despite our adult urges to suppress it, laughter comes naturally to us. But as Reverend Susan Sparks points out in *Laugh Your Way to Grace: Reclaiming the Spiritual Power of Humor*, we have to choose to use it:

> As adults, it is easy to see ourselves as pessimists or to believe that we have no sense of humor. Life can certainly beat the joy right out of us. But no matter how dormant our joy, the one thing life can't take is our innate ability to laugh. Laughter is a choice. In truth, human beings are [hardwired] to laugh.[3]

In order for us to more easily choose laughter, we must be able to see the hilariousness in our own lives; to see who we *really* are, rather than who we think we are, and be comfortable with the complete package. Say it with me: "I am humorous. I am the butt of a good number of jokes."

Laughter's Saving Grace

Christian theologian G. K. Chesterton said, "Angels can fly because they take themselves lightly."[4] I affirm the truth in this statement because learning to laugh at myself gave my calling to be a pastor its wings.

It was Easter morning in 1985, and the church where I worked as a seminary intern was packed. I got up to lead the congregation in a responsive reading of a Psalm. After reading each of my lines, I looked up and made eye contact with the congregation. I wanted them to feel I was present with them. Halfway through the reading, after looking into the eyes of the congregation, I promptly lost my place. I panicked and read the first line my eyes fell upon—the congregation's line. Then, in a surprising act of corporate grace, they read their next line. Completely discombobulated, I read their line again. The congregation, now realizing I was completely lost, read my next line. We had switched places, and now I was reading their lines. That's when you could hear it coming—a low rumble of growing giggles. I read the last line, which should have been theirs, with a thank-God-that's-over "Amen!" The congregation erupted with laughter. And so did I—I had blown it so badly! The pastor, who was supposed to do whatever came next, could not get out of his chair he was laughing so hard. Tears were running down our faces. It took us five minutes to return to the order of worship! The entire congregation had a smile for the rest of the service.

But there's more to the story. Two years later I had graduated from seminary and was looking for my first call as a pastor. The Presbyterian process asked every would-be pastor to complete an extensive Personal Information Form (PIF), replete with past work history and ministry experiences; education; essay responses to umpteen questions about theology, style of leadership, and the most pressing issues facing the church; and a one-page cover letter to grab the attention of prospective churches. If that wasn't enough pressure, there were more pastors looking for calls than positions available across the country. I had read several of my friends' cover letters, highlighting their summa cum laudes in education and their successes in ministry, and my list of accomplishments just didn't match up. What was I going to do? I decided to tell the story of my Easter blunder, and I sent out my PIF.

About a week later I received a phone call from the chair of an associate pastor search committee, who said, "Tim, we've looked at hundreds of PIFs over the past six months. We had just whittled our list down to three finalists, when I received one final stack. I had looked at so many of these things that I'd get about one paragraph in and say, 'Nope,' and I'd toss the PIF to the side. I went through the first ten in about five minutes—I was so tired of candidates tooting their own horn! Then I came across your cover letter. Couldn't put it down. You took a big risk! But you showed you could laugh at yourself, that you didn't take yourself too seriously. We could use some of that around here. The committee voted to expand our list of candidates to four. When can you fly out for an interview?" Laughter turned into my first call as a pastor.

Laughter: A Sign of Wisdom

Learning to laugh at ourselves is a sign of growth, maturity, and deep wisdom. It demonstrates that we have gained a certain amount of freedom from our inner critic, the perfectionism reflected in much of society, and our ego. Knowing that we are imperfect, prone to making mistakes, and subject to our own blind spots and foibles means we are no longer trapped by failure or error. Prominent modernist writer Katherine Mansfield said, "When we can begin to take our failures nonseriously, it means we are ceasing to be afraid of them. It is of immense importance to learn to laugh at ourselves."[5] The American actress Ethel Barrymore concurred when she said, "You grow up the day you have your first real laugh—at yourself."[6]

As Reverend Sparks notes, learning to laugh at ourselves is a sign that we are growing spiritually:

> If our spiritual path is to have any life, it needs to be shaken out a bit and given room to grow. Laughter tends to do just that. It shakes up our "roots" and brings air and energy into tired, worn souls. If we give ourselves permission to feel and play and laugh on our own terms, who knows—we might learn something new.[7]

Abraham and Sarah in the Hebrew Bible laugh at themselves when God tells Abraham that Sarah is about to have a baby (Genesis 17:15–17). Abraham does not just chuckle; he rolls on the ground in a fit of laughter. *Oh, that's a good one, God. Yeah, right!* Later, Sarah does the same thing as she overhears God speaking to Abraham (Genesis 18:9–15). God responds by questioning the reason for Sarah's laughter: "Is anything too wonderful for the Lord?" We often misinterpret this response. We think God is offended by Abraham's laughter, so we hear God's words filled with anger: "No, your wife will bear a son and his name shall be Isaac!" But what if we hear it differently? "No, Abraham, your wife will bear a son and—*magnifique!*—you will name him, 'Isaac'—which, Abe, if you happen to know your Hebrew, means *He laughs!*" Can you think of a better way to remind this old couple of God's goodness?

Does Jesus laugh? There is a long-running debate about this, which actually began back in the medieval Christian church. It's true, there isn't a single text in the Christian Scriptures that explicitly says that Jesus laughs, but that doesn't mean he doesn't. In *The Humor of Christ*, Quaker theologian Elton Trueblood suggests that Jesus must have laughed, just as any talented storyteller would. But most of us miss the humor in the gospels, either because we're so familiar with the tales and parables or because we can't see through Jesus's particular brand of sarcasm. But just consider the image of threading a camel through the eye of a needle (Matthew 19:24; Mark 10:25). Or Matthew 7:3, "Why do you see the speck in your neighbor's eye, but do not notice the log in your own eye?" That's funny stuff.

Sometimes, in order to see Jesus laugh, we have to read into the gospels. In Matthew 24:1–12, we have one of the few examples of Jesus getting bested, and it may be a watershed moment for him. His ministry is in full swing, but he knows his teachings will get him in trouble. This is serious. Suddenly, a Canaanite woman cries aloud for Jesus to have mercy on her daughter. But she is playing in a patriarchal ballpark. This woman (strike one) is of a despised race (strike two) and has a daughter, not a son (strike three, you're out!). The story says Jesus *ignores* her! But she persists. The disciples can't make her go away, so they ask Jesus to send her away. Jesus tells her God's mercy is for the chosen people, the lost sheep of Israel, not her. She pleads again, this time on her knees. Jesus responds, "It is not fair to take the children's food and throw it to the dogs."

This is such a low blow! First, Jesus calls the woman, her daughter, and her people *dogs*, which in first-century Palestine are seen as dirty, despised creatures. Second, Jesus refers to Jews as *children* to emphasize the contrast: Jews are not dogs. Third, Jesus says it is not *fair*. A quick examination of Jesus's parables and stories exposes the irony—if not hilarity—here:

- The story of the landowner who hires workers to work in his fields: He pays the ones who work one hour the same as those who work all day! Not fair.
- The parable of the father with two sons: The elder son does everything right and never has a party thrown for him, but the prodigal son, after wasting his inheritance, comes home to have a feast thrown for him! Not fair.

Jesus's *entire message* has been about God's amazing grace, which goes far beyond what's fair! Now he's saying it's not fair to help this woman's daughter?

Jesus gets caught up in the seriousness of his ministry and loses sight of the message. But this Canaanite woman is sharp! She says, "Yes, Lord. Yet even the dogs eat the crumbs that fall from their master's table." I can hear Homer Simpson in the background—"Doh!" Jesus may have gotten upset here. She challenges him, defies him, argues with him, and does so in front of his disciples. He can't lose face! But Jesus gets the joke, and he knows it is on him. He recognizes that the very thing for which he will soon get crucified is the very thing he is denying this woman. And he laughs—at himself! He exclaims, "Woman, great is your faith!" And her daughter is healed.

Dig Deep, It's There

Just as we have to read into the gospels to find the humor, we need to dig deep into ourselves to reclaim our childlike ability to laugh, especially at ourselves. As Dr. Grieger advises:

> Keep an eye out for life's absurdities. When you run across them, let yourself be amused. Notice how sports fans take their team's losing as dire as the specter of death. Observe the gentleman who fumes because his steak is not cooked exactly to his liking. Appreciate the silly affectations of the people willing to parade themselves around on those TV reality shows. Life's little circuses offer an endless supply of humor, especially when noticed in yourself.[8]

What we find when we do this is the outlandishness of the grace of God, who does impossible things with impossible people, and turns death into life. Blessed is the one who gets that joke, for no one, not one of us, gets what we deserve—we get vastly more.

Practices

Think of Something Funny

This sounds almost too easy, but it works! Get comfortable, relax, and close your eyes. Think back to something funny that happened—to you, a friend, anyone. Allow the full memory to return and let yourself respond to it. You may find this is all you need to experience the laughter and humor in the present. Let yourself really feel the laughter again, and then notice other accompanying feelings. Laughter, especially shared laughter or laughter directed at yourself, is accompanied by joy, love, freedom, and gratitude.

Laughing at Yourself

Take some time to look at yourself as objectively as possible, as if seeing yourself through the eyes of someone else. Consider your habits, facial expressions, typical sayings, personality traits, disparities between your words and actions, beliefs, relationships, and idiosyncrasies. What's funny about you? How can you get to a place where you can laugh about it?

10 Recess!

PLAYING YOUR WAY TO LIFE AND PURPOSE

Deep play allows one to feel quintessentially alive,
heartbeat by heartbeat, in the eternal present.
The here and now becomes a pop-up storybook,
full of surprises, in which everything looms. It
returns us to the openness of childhood.

DIANE ACKERMAN

Every man and woman should live life accordingly,
and play the noblest games ... What, then, is the
right way of living? Life must be lived as play.

PLATO

I took a trip with three friends to Puerto Rico one summer. Vivian, who lived in Puerto Rico, acted as our tour guide. We were always going somewhere new and interesting. Near the end of our stay, Vivian took us to El Yunque, one of the highest peaks in Puerto Rico. The day started out with clear skies, but as we drove higher into the rain forest, the clouds thickened. By the time we entered the park it was raining. We pulled into a parking lot and waited, but the rain kept pouring, now in thick sheets. We were all disappointed, particularly Vivian. But then suddenly a smile stretched across Vivian's face and her eyes grew wide. She looked at each of us, then flung the car door open and stepped out into the deluge. She was instantly drenched, and began laughing hysterically. We watched, stunned, as she pranced in the rain and splashed in the shallow lake that had been a parking lot. She raised her hands and face up to the sky, then looked at us in the car and said, "C'mon out! It's only water!" And with that, we all joined her. In seconds, we were soaked to the bone, wetter than fish, and happy as clams.

Play: It's Not Just Goofing Around

Vivian, displaying a capacity for seeing outside the bounds of normative adult thinking and behavior, turned disappointment into one of the most memorable moments of our trip. She captured the spirit of play, where the everyday becomes enhanced, where dead ends become delightful detours, where ennui turns into enchantment. Play is the ability to change the equal sign in an equation to a "maybe." Maybe there is another way to see this, maybe there is another way to do this, maybe there is another way to respond. Just because it's raining cats and dogs does not mean we must stay in the car. Playfulness makes the world and our lives a more enchanted place.

But play is not simply for enchantment. Or, from another perspective, enchantment is not just play. Play is serious business, and if we want to be serious about our business, we must learn to play. Through play we learn how to live our lives; the ability to play enables us to live well. Diane Ackerman, in her wonderful book *Deep Play*, writes,

> In a dangerous world, where dramas change daily, survival belongs to the agile, not the idle. We may think of play as optional, a casual activity. But play is fundamental to evolution. Without play, humans and many other animals would perish.[1]

Both animals and humans play, but humans take play to another level. As a recent article in the *New York Times* made clear, whereas animals use play as training for life, humans use play to develop the imagination.

> Kittens may pretend to be cats fighting, but they will not pretend to be children; children, by contrast, will readily pretend to be cats or kittens—and then to be Hannah Montana, followed by Spider-Man saving the day. And in doing so, they develop some of humanity's most consequential faculties. They learn the art, pleasure and

power of hypothesis—of imagining new possibilities. And serious students of play believe that this helps make the species great.[2]

Losing Play to Established Patterns

How we play changes as we mature. Playing just to play, which we do as children, turns into competition as adults. Playmates become opposing teammates, creating an us-versus-them mentality. Winning at all costs becomes the highest value, with egos, reputations, and often money at stake. Dr. Alison Gopnik, leading children's psychology researcher and author of books such as *The Scientist in the Crib* and *The Philosophical Baby*, identifies the difference between the way children play and the way adults play as exploring versus exploiting:

> To exploit, one leans heavily on lessons and often unconscious rules learned earlier in life—so-called prior biases. These biases are useful to adults because they save time and reduce error: By going to the restaurant you know is good instead of the new place across town, you increase the chance that you'll enjoy the evening.
>
> Most adults are slow to set such biases aside for the sake of exploration; young children fling them away like bad fruit.[3]

This distinction at the heart of play—between being willing to explore and see what happens and a tendency to exploit and rely on biases—was brought home to me in the very writing of this chapter. I had just finished the rough draft, and at the heart of it was a story of my experience of play at a weeklong festival that led to a profoundly transformational experience for me. I knew the story would be risky for me as an author to tell, but it felt right. I anticipated a positive response from my editor.

My editor's response was not to my liking. She said she didn't think that story was suitable for my book. I was somewhat taken aback and found myself moping around, feeling sorry for myself. But then I pushed back, saying I thought it was important to be self-revealing and I wanted my editor to give the story a chance. My arms were crossed, my brow was firmly set into a deep furrow; I was sure my story was the only way to go.

So while I waited for her response, I worked on fine-tuning chapter 9, "Laughter and a Sense of Humor: Grace's Daily Dietary Requirement."

After adding the story of little Maggie's profound impact on a meeting of the board of elders, I suddenly had an epiphany and began to laugh at myself. My email to my editor says it best:

> I must tell you what happened to me yesterday. I was working a bit on rewriting the first part of the chapter on laughter, the story of little Maggie's hand slap on the table and its impact on the meeting of the board of elders. As I remembered Maggie's laughter, and how it broke open a tense meeting, I suddenly saw my own seriousness about my experience of play at the festival and my insistence on keeping it in the book, and I burst out laughing! My whole mood lightened up; I began to play with different ways I might write the chapter, and make it even better. And then I thought of using this very experience as a way to illustrate our need for childlike play in chapter 10!

After I sent this email to my editor, I reflected back on lessons learned as an artist. Many times I had worked hard on a painting, only to find that I'd painted myself into a corner and didn't like where the painting was going. It often took a couple of days, if not weeks, to address this. First I would try to "fix" the painting, but continue going in the same direction. When that didn't work (it usually made it worse), I would simply stare at it for hours, if not days. Finally, I would begin to play with the painting. I had to let go of the present form and be willing to try something different. I remember, in a sudden spirit of play, once blotting out three-quarters of a 36 by 60-inch painting with red and suddenly seeing a completely different painting emerge from that moment of playful inspiration!

How easy it is for adults to hold on to our biases, take ourselves too seriously, and paint ourselves into a corner. A child's willingness to explore the many possibilities and see what might happen is an invitation for us to develop our own sense of deep play with our lives. Deep play invites us to wholeness, opens us to our soul, and encourages us to thrive.

Reaching beyond Ourselves—Playfully

The exhortation by Jesus to become childlike invites us to be less serious about ourselves and instead seek the profound through play. According to

Nika Quirk, a masterful InterPlay improv leader and EveryDay Leadership coach, play is indeed a spiritual practice. In her work, Quirk encourages people to "hold life lightly and meaningfully." She stresses that we don't have to shut down our playful imaginative selves to find meaning in our world. Giving ourselves permission to embrace the lighter side of life can open up a channel for our spirits to soar.

Quirk describes play as a profound act. Play becomes the way to connect to, and fill, the often magical space from which we create. Recognizing the deep meaning and healing that can be found as we connect to our playful, creative, and inspirational selves can be a truly spiritual process.[4]

Play becomes a spiritual practice when we begin to recognize moments where we need to connect to our expansive selves. It becomes a spiritual practice when we must consciously shift our awareness from what may be self-limiting to what is self-fulfilling. Knowing our relationship to play—this lighter side of life—and what helps us connect to this transformational place is a key element in our spiritual practice. How and when we play has a powerful impact on the way we live our lives.

When we bring playfulness to our vocations, relationships, responsibilities, desires, and dreams, we open ourselves up to the depths in every one of these areas, making them more meaningful and soul-nourishing. As Plato suggests, "What, then, is the right way of living? Life must be lived as play."[5] At their heart, spirituality and religion are heightened forms of playing with the mystery we call ourselves and the mystery we call God. As Diane Ackerman writes,

> The basis for all religions is our natural ability to enter altered states of consciousness, in which we feel heightened awareness and a sense of revelation, insight, fearful awe, and harmony. Religion offers a passionate form of deep play, whose peak moments are as subjective as they are intense.[6]

Just Play!

My girlfriend, Julie, told me recently about a conversation she had with her six-year-old daughter, Dezi.

"Dezi, I know three people now who are writing books."

"Nana is one!" Dezi exclaimed.

"That's right," Julie said, "and Pete, too."

"Who's the other person?" Dezi asked.

"Tim. Do you want to know the title of his book?"

"What is it?" she asked.

"*Like a Child.*"

Dezi's eyes grew wide. "Oh, you'll have to get that for me when it comes out!"

"It's a book for adults."

Dezi had a quizzical look on her face. "Oh, to teach them to be more like kids?"

"Yes. What advice would you give to adults to become more like children?"

Dezi said, "Play more!!"

When we find ourselves stuck and disappointed, and the clouds are raining on our plans, we might remind ourselves of Vivian's playful, childlike perspective and Dezi's sound advice. How can we jump more into life and play?

Practices

Go Out and Play!

This may be the simplest of practices! Do something you love to do. Gather friends to play cards, a board game, or charades. Play tennis, basketball, ping-pong, darts, Frisbee, tag, hide-and-seek—whatever. Go to a park, find a swing, and swing! Do anything that feels like play to you and enter into it fully.

Afterward, find a quiet time and place to reflect on your experience of play.

What feelings and thoughts arose?

What challenges did you face?

What invitations do you notice?

Turn Everything into a Game

This attitude can be applied in all sorts of situations. Take whatever it is you are doing and turn it into a game. For example, say it's your turn to cook tonight. Instead of "cooking," let yourself play "celebrity chef." You have a staff meeting tomorrow to plan strategy for the upcoming month. How can you play at creating a productive, meaningful month?

Take a moment to consider the tasks and events of the next few days. Play around in your imagination with ways you could put a fun twist on each of the tasks and events that come to mind. Then choose one or two ideas that particularly bring you joy and make them happen!

No matter what you are doing, ask yourself, and invite others who are with you, how you might bring to it a sense of playfulness, curiosity, and exploration.

11 Inside Out, Outside In

LIVING AN UNDIVIDED LIFE

With the dropping away of the hope or desire to get it right, I caught a glimpse of something new; I sank into a direct if brief experience of who—or perhaps more accurately what—I am. It took my breath away.
ORIAH MOUNTAIN DREAMER

We have to dare to be ourselves, however frightening or strange that self may prove to be.
MAY SARTON

The privilege of a lifetime is to become who you truly are.
C. G. JUNG

I stood next to the baptismal font in front of the packed congregation. A new family had been attending regularly and I was about to baptize their two daughters, Britt, age three, and Courtney, age six. We had practiced earlier in the week, so I expected everything to go smoothly. I asked Britt, "Can I pick you up and baptize you?" She said, "No!" and crossed her arms.

I looked quickly at her parents and they were shocked. I got down on my knees, now eye-to-eye with Britt, and said, "Would you like to stand here like a big girl, like your sister did, and I'll baptize you that way?" Britt stood up taller and said, "Yes, please."

From Divided Life to Möbius Bliss

Children, as we have noted, have a wonderful way of being simply all that they are. Little, if anything, is held back. They are refreshingly unpretentious. We adults were once that way, too, but gradually we learned there were acceptable and unacceptable thoughts, emotions, attitudes, and behaviors. Many of us formed our sense of self by taking on much of what was acceptable and repressing much of what was unacceptable. This is the natural process of growing up, but there is a shadow side to it, as I expressed in a song I wrote, inspired by a Rainer Maria Rilke poem:

We come of age as masks,
Made up of part pomp and part circumstance,
Our God is better, our way is best.
To be embarrassed is worse than the kiss of death.

By the time we come of age, we end up living a divided life between who we are perceived to be and who we really are. For many of us, this results in living much of our lives with our false self out in front. Richard Rohr, in *Immortal Diamond*, identifies four major splits from reality that we have all made in varying degrees to create our false self:

1. We split from our shadow self and pretend to be our idealized self.

2. We split our mind from our body and soul and live in our minds.

3. We split life from death and try to live our life without any "death."

4. We split ourselves from other selves and try to live apart, superior, and separate.[1]

To a great degree, each of these splits is a response to fear and anxiety, a way to protect ourselves. It hurts to acknowledge our imperfections, shortcomings, and failings, but in order to deny them, we must ignore the urges of our bodies and spirits, the reality of our mortality, and our place within the community. The protection we create becomes its own prison.

In *A Hidden Wholeness: The Journey toward an Undivided Life*, Parker J. Palmer uses a simple strip of paper to illustrate how we build protective walls to forge a prison throughout the four phases of life. One side of the strip of paper represents our *outside* life—what others see and experience of us—and the other side represents our *inside* life—what we feel, think, desire, intuit, sense, believe, and doubt.

In life's first phase, when we enter this world as a child, there is no difference between the inside and the outside. As Palmer says, "This is why most of us love to be around infants and young children: what we see is what we get."[2]

In phase two, when we leave childhood and enter adolescence and early adulthood, we begin building a protective wall between the outside world and our inner world. Imagine holding a strip of paper in both hands, level with the surface of a table, as if it were a wall or fence. Behind this fence are the vulnerable, fragile parts of ourselves we do not show to the world. On the front side of the strip of paper are the parts of ourselves we feel comfortable showing the world, or feel we need to show in order to survive or achieve. The thicker the wall of protection, the harder it is to let it down. What we hide from others, we soon hide from ourselves.

Living behind a wall has at least three consequences, according to Palmer:

1. Our inner light and gifts cannot inform our life and work in the world.

2. Our inner darkness cannot receive the light that exists in the world.

3. People close to us become wary of the gap between the onstage and offstage self.[3]

The discomfort of living a divided life, when we are open to its message, helps us move into phase three, which Palmer describes as a desire for our inner values to govern our outward life. To symbolize this, Palmer invites us to take the ends of the strip of paper and join them together to make a circle, like a corral. To live out of and have a center provides a "plumb line for the choices I make about my life."[4] But developing a center in this way can result in a circling of the wagons, where our inner truth creates a sense of inclusion and exclusion, an us-versus-them mentality.

> When we use our truth to create such divisions, we fall far short of the open-hearted engagement with the world that all the great spiritual traditions advocate. Now the circle of phase three is no more than the wall of phase two in disguise.[5]

The final phase is illustrated by holding the ends of the strip of paper in both hands, giving one end a half-twist, and then rejoining the ends. You now have what is known as a Möbius strip. Take the tip of your finger and trace the outside surface of the Möbius strip. You will find that suddenly you are tracing on the inside of the Möbius strip, and if you keep going, you are again on the outside. There is no inside or outside of a Möbius strip; it is one continuous surface, indicating that,

> whatever is inside us continually flows outward to help form, or deform, the world—and whatever is outside us continually flows inward to help form, or deform, our lives. The Möbius strip is like life itself: here, ultimately, there is only one reality.[6]

The Möbius strip is a wonderful illustration of what it means to become like a child as an adult. Our inner life affects the world, and the world's life affects our inner life, so how might we be more deeply aware of both?

For us to become like children, we must realize that the inside and the outside are continually looping back in on each other, a dance that allows us to co-create—with God and with our fellow humans—a world worth living in.

A Complex Self Is a Whole Self

Part of the problem with living an undivided life is that we often hold the false assumption that we are a simple, and therefore, a singular self. We set tight parameters on who we are and repress, hide, and project onto others the parts of us that don't fit within these narrow borders.

When I decided in my sophomore year of college to go into the ministry, I thought it was such an important vocation that it had to consume all my time, become my sole identity, and result in a life of sterling character. I felt the pressure of conforming to a high ideal, and when I would read the writings of the Apostle Paul I felt that I had a long way to go to reach this singular sense of self. Looking back, I see how hard I was on myself and how I hid parts of myself from others because I didn't want them to see my "bad side." I also hid that "bad side" from myself.

But living an undivided life does not mean we are not full of paradoxes, complexities, and conundrums. A closer look at ourselves reveals that we are enormously complex. (Todd Christensen, a five-time Pro Bowl tight end who played most of his career with the Oakland Raiders, wrote poetry, for example.) The undivided life challenges us to admit that this complexity exists, and to bring all that we are into our relationships, vocation, and the totality of our life. Accepting all that we are, accepting ourselves, changes everything.

Accepting Our Complexities

In *Soul Mates: Honoring the Mystery of Love and Relationship*, best-selling author Thomas Moore describes the moment such self-acceptance struck home for him. He had been through a tumultuous year, and wasn't able to understand the changes taking place in his life, when a friend gave him a book that contained Paul Tillich's famous sermon "You Are Accepted." This sermon focuses on the self-division and separation within all of us, and the effect this division has on our relationships and our lives. Tillich said, "When the old compulsions reign within us as they have for decades, when despair destroys all joy and courage, sometimes at that moment a wave of light breaks into our darkness, and it is as though a voice were saying: 'You are accepted. You are accepted.'"[7]

For Moore, one takeaway from Tillich's sermon was that acceptance begins when we envision owning our imperfections and what that may mean for understanding ourselves and deepening our relationships. When we imagine this,

> Suddenly, things look different. I am the same person I have always been, and yet I am not. The world hasn't changed, and yet it feels different. The difficult truth to learn is that true change takes place in the imagination, and knowing this has everything to do with developing a good, intimate relationship to our own soul and the souls of others.[8]

Part of living an undivided life is taking a close look at the parts of ourselves that we have buried, denied, minimized, and paid little attention to. In *Stripping Down: The Art of Spiritual Restoration*, spiritual teacher Donna Schaper likens this work to restoring old wooden furniture. In order to know your true self, your singular self, you have to scrape away the accumulated layers of paint and dirt and see what is underneath.

Every now and then I have to take a really hard look at the illusions I've built up in myself and my society, see what I've gotten myself into. Illusions? Yes, illusions; the excess baggage I carry around, the unnecessary, the socially expected, all that keeps me living off center too long.... I have to discover the original under all these coats I've added, strip away all the cynicism and anger I've built up, get rid of the junk I've taken on, defy my disappointments, and find what is real again.[9]

Sometimes Our Complexities Find Us

Sometimes we don't have to search for the hidden, minimalized parts of us; they find us. As David Whyte suggests in *The Heart Aroused: Poetry and the Preservation of the Soul in Corporate America*, "We will always be hunted by what we have most denied in ourselves."[10]

All through elementary school I loved math and art. My older sister, who hated math but was an amazing artist, claimed the identity of the family artist, so I chose to focus on sports and math. However, a profound, life-changing religious experience in college made my life's course clear: I would go into ordained ministry. Even when my art professor, as I mentioned earlier, pleaded with me to become an art major, I stayed my course.

But years later, and well into my vocation as a pastor, a gnawing dissatisfaction showed up as a desire for creative expression. A girlfriend gave me a simple watercolor set. I made my first painting. That was fun. I did another, and another, and another! Soon I had a show in a café, and I sold my first painting. Could this also be what I was meant to do? But then a painting came out of me that surprised and shocked me—a stoic, overly voluptuous, female nude. I took the painting with me to an artists' group, and their feedback to me about my painting was insightful. It was as if this painting were the creative part of me hunting me down and grabbing my attention: "I am here. I am not going away. You need to pay attention to me, because I am you. What are you going to do with me?"

Whole Self, Whole Life

My encounter with that painting—and the hidden side of myself that it hinted at—was the beginning of a growing realization that though my spiritual life and the ministry were important parts of who I was, that was not all of me. My soul was not going to settle for anything but all of me, and that included my creative side—expressive, curious, adventurous—that showed up as Eros, hunting me down, inviting me to live a fuller, richer, broader life. My life.

When we accept ourselves this way, embracing latent gifts and talents, our complexities, and even our faults and failings, we find we no longer need the wall we created to keep inside and outside separate. We move closer to becoming like a child, where distinctions between inside and outside fade away, and we move toward the wholeness that is ours.

Practices

Return to Childhood

Sit comfortably and breathe deeply. When you are ready, revisit your childhood. Recall what you loved to do and the things you were genuinely interested in.

What did you love to do when you were, say, five years old?

Who or what did you pretend to be?

What was your favorite game to play?

What was your first big accomplishment and how did that feel?

Consider how these things, interests, and activities might reflect inherent aspects of who you are today. How might you embrace and express those parts of yourself now?

Act Like You're a Kid Again

Take what you discovered in your "Return to Childhood" and put it into practice.

For example, let's say you loved swinging on a swing as a kid. Find some time on a Saturday or Sunday, and take yourself to a park that has swings. Now swing for 15 or 20 minutes.

As you swing, what feelings stir in you?

What thoughts, images, or memories arise?

Notice any judgments you might have about what you're doing, and the feelings and thoughts that come to you. Where do those judgments come from?

How can you let the judgments go and simply return to swinging?

You can do this practice with riding a bike, swimming, playing music, arranging building blocks, jumping on a trampoline, drawing, creating stories, and more.

Möbius Strip Meditation

Cut a strip of paper 11 to 14 inches long and 2 inches wide, and set it down on a desk or flat surface so that the 2-inch edge is pointing at you, and it looks like a thin skyscraper. Starting at the top, write down all the things you can think of that have the most influence on you from the outside (examples: media, spouse, role at work, etc.). Then turn the strip of paper over, and, again starting at the top, write down all the things you can think of that come from inside you (examples: specific feelings, resentments, anger, gratitude, hopes, self-doubts, confidence, desires and longings, talents, etc.).

When you're finished, take the strip of paper by the 2-inch ends, give one end a twist, and tape the ends together, making a Möbius strip. Set aside 20 or 30 minutes to look at everything you wrote down, and contemplate how you might be more aware of how the "outside" things affect you.

If you are happy with them, how might you collaborate with those things to enhance your life?

If you are not happy with those effects, how might you curtail or limit their impact on you?

Do the same thing with the "inside" things.

Are you happy with their effect on your outside or public life?

What can you do to enhance or limit their effect?

12 It Takes a Long Time to Become Young

TRANSFORMING A LIFE, CULTIVATING A SOUL

The more we allow ourselves to unfold,
the less likely we are to unravel.

RABBI IRWIN KULA

Rather than being a fall away from beauty, aging
can be the revelation of beauty, the time when
the inherent radiance becomes visible.

JOHN O'DONOHUE

Throughout this book, I have used words and phrases like *true self* and *soul* to express that we are more than the brushstrokes of environment, genetics, and nurture applied to a blank-canvas self. We come into this world with a self that is ours and ours alone—unique, particular, and mysterious. But in our desire to grow up, mature, become adults, we start to think the mask we've donned is who we are supposed to be. Then, when we have finally "grown up," we realize that much of who we really are has been left behind or buried under various masks and roles we play. Our true self can sometimes seem so far away as to

117

be unrecoverable. But we can reconnect with our authentic selves from childhood because that knowledge of who we truly are never leaves us. As Parker J. Palmer writes,

> I find it fascinating that the very old, who often forget a great deal, may recover vivid memories of childhood, of that time in their lives when they were most like themselves. They are brought back to their birthright by the abiding core of selfhood they carry within—a core made more visible, perhaps, by the way aging can strip away whatever is not truly us.[1]

To reclaim our selfhood, we must grow up again, become like children, and consciously embrace all that it means to be childlike. As the artist Pablo Picasso suggests, "It takes a long time to become young."

Welcoming a Spiritual Rebirth

In the Gospel of John, Jesus tells Nicodemus, "No one can see the kingdom of God without being born from above" (or, as it's more commonly translated, "born again"). Nicodemus is incredulous. "How can anyone be born after having grown old? Can one enter a second time into the mother's womb and be born?" Jesus answers him, "Truly, no one can enter the kingdom of God without being born of water and Spirit" (3:3–5). Jesus is urging us, in part, to return to our essence, our true self. He is encouraging us to embrace a spiritual rebirth.

Our own childhood may prove an invaluable source of that spiritual rebirth. Thomas Moore, in *Dark Nights of the Soul: A Guide to Finding Your Way Through Life's Ordeals*, writes,

> The gap between your adult self and the spirit of the child can be overcome in simple, concrete ways. You have to remember that the child qualities you need as an adult are connected with your own childhood. You have to redeem that childhood and come to peace with it.[2]

Moore cites the experience of Carl Jung as an example of someone connecting with his childhood to cultivate his own soul. In a difficult period in his late thirties, during World War I, Jung had a powerful memory of himself at age eleven, playing with blocks and stones. He began playing with blocks and stones during his lunch break and at the end of the day after seeing his patients. This "work" made him feel uncomfortable, for he was being childish, yet it proved vital for him:

> This moment was a turning point in my fate, but I gave in only after endless resistances and with a sense of resignation. For it was a painfully humiliating experience to realize that there was nothing to be done except play childish games.[3]

For me, writing was a vital channel to my childhood self. In seventh grade I wrote a story for my English class. It was titled "Murder on 63rd Street." I don't recall any details of the story itself, other than it was set in New York City, but I remember how writing the story made me feel: I felt at home. When the teacher read it aloud to the class, I felt in some way that I was being listened to and read. Many years later, when I found out I hadn't been accepted into the PhD program I'd applied to, I began writing a novel, and I came upon that feeling again—*this is me and I need to embrace this part of myself.*

The Soul's Journey: Prepare for the Long Haul

To become like a child, a lifelong process, is to purposefully become vulnerable and malleable again. It is as much letting go and shedding layers of cultural sediment built up over time as it is allowing our essence, our soul, our individual self to emerge out from under the conventional and socially acceptable roles we play. Becoming like a child, we find our own medicine, as Native Americans put it, or, as the knights in search of the Holy Grail view their mission, we enter the inner forest where there is no path to follow but the one we forge ourselves. This is not an ego-driven quest; it is something the soul does. The only question is this: Will we join the quest or refuse to enter the woods?

As Pope Francis entered the second year of his papacy, surrounded by accolades from across the globe for his open stance and emphasis on compassion, social leader and activist Timothy Shriver cautioned us to pay attention to the real message of Pope Francis because he was not just asking for economic or social compassion, but inner transformation. Shriver writes,

Most people are applauding Francis's call to change the Catholic hierarchy, and many are welcoming his challenge to attack economic inequality. But his call to change isn't just about the social justice we seek for others or the reform of outdated Catholic insularity. It's also about the deep and often painful work of changing ourselves from the inside out. The Hebrew prophet Joel captured the challenge of the inner life clearly: "Change your heart, not your garments." Still, changing one's heart isn't easy.[4]

The description in the gospels of Jesus being driven by the Spirit into the wilderness to be tempted is a metaphor for our own necessary grappling with our deepest identity. Will we be all these things family, friends, society, and religion expect us to be? Or will we divest ourselves of the external and temporary, and invest in the internal and eternal?

The length of Jesus's temptation—forty days, a direct connection to the forty years the Israelites wandered in the wilderness—is a metaphor for the length of this soul journey. Being reborn is not simply a moment's transformation, but also a lifelong journey. Irish poet John O'Donohue describes this process as the heart of the mystical tradition:

It is not about building protectionist armor of prayer and religion; it is, rather, the courage of absolute divestment. In the sheer vulnerability of Nothingness everything becomes possible in a new way, but there is an immense temptation to flee back to the shelter of old complacency. Now could be the most important moment in life to steel our courage and enter the risk of change.[5]

Embracing Sunshine and Shadow

Cultivating a soul is not a matter of perfection or progress, achievement or improvement. It is returning, unfolding, uncovering, and releasing our inherent uniqueness, our true self, in all its complexity, beauty, and strangeness. Our childhood holds glimpses and memories of the essence of our souls before we were squeezed into molds, impressed by heroes, and desired to *belong* more than *be*. Becoming like a child is the willingness to discover and embrace the immense world of our soul, and to recognize the immense world that is our neighbor. That means embracing our shadow self—the parts of us that appear strange and unknown—and finding the gifts these parts of us offer.

My mother says that when I was a toddler I used to love to get into the cupboard under the stove, take out the pots and pans, and spin the lids on the floor to see what would happen. Similarly, I have been·"spinning things to see what happens" in all kinds of ways as I've lived my adult life. When the strange and surprising erotic painting came out of me, mentioned in chapter 11, "Inside Out, Outside In: Living an Undivided Life," I slowly began to realize that the strange image I'd painted was an invitation for me to move toward a fuller, richer, more passionate life, and to bring all my gifts into play in creating and living my life. Just like dreams and their strange imagery, the parts of our lives and souls we have not yet embraced, lived into, and expressed will appear to us in strange images or as strange behavior, in order to get our attention, urging us to recognize that something of great value needs to be welcomed into our lives.

It is precisely here, on this long journey of becoming, that the many qualities and characteristics of a child that we have explored in this book come into play. Becoming like a child, embracing this unfolding of your true self over time, calls for a deep sense of trust in yourself and in God, an openness to wonder at the fires that burn in your soul and flare up in the world, a willingness to live closer to the truth of all that you are and are not, a willingness to see yourself with the eyes of innocence, a heart of compassion and forgiveness, and a willingness to begin anew. These child-like qualities then begin to inform what wholeness and holiness mean. John O'Donohue writes,

> When you trust yourself enough to discover and integrate your strangeness, you bestow a gift on yourself. Rather than annulling a complex part of your heart, which would continue to haunt you, you have thrown your arms around yourself to embrace who you are. This is at the heart of holiness. Holiness is not complacent refuge in the glasshouse of pale pieties. To be holy is to enter the dense beauty of passionate complexity.[6]

The kingdom of God, for Jesus, is the realm where wholeness and holiness hold true for individuals and community. The parties where Jesus gathers around a table with all kinds of people—the religiously pure and politically

elite, the peasants, tax collectors, lepers, outcasts, and sinners—is not acci-
dental or incidental to his message. These gatherings are a metaphor for
embracing not only the acceptable parts of ourselves but also the parts of
ourselves we repress or hide from ourselves and others. In the kingdom of
God, all of *us* (every one) are and *all* of us (every part of us) is embraced,
accepted, and nourished.

Your Childlike Self Is Calling

Lying on his deathbed, Reb Zusya was very upset and crying, tears stream-
ing down his face. His students asked with great concern, "Reb Zusya, why
are you upset? Why are you crying? Are you afraid when you die you will
be asked why you were not more like Moses?"

Reb Zusya replied, "I am not afraid that the Holy One will ask me 'Zusya,
why were you not more like Moses?' Rather, I fear that the Holy One will
say, 'Zusya, why were you not more like Zusya?'"[7]

We are, each one of us, born with a uniqueness all our own, our very
own soul with its own essence, and it takes a long time to recognize its
presence, listen to its voice, trust its wisdom, and let it unfold into our life.
In doing so, we become like children—and surprisingly find that we have
arrived in the kingdom of God, the place we have always lived but often
do not recognize.

Practices

Not Moses, Me

Each one of us has a list of people we look up to, admire, and respect:
heroes, mentors, exemplars, and idols. Identify the people in your life you
have tried to be like and emulate.

What qualities have they helped you develop?

In what ways have their qualities or traits overshadowed your own
gifts, talents, and characteristics?

What would it mean to be truly you, instead of being like one of the people you look up to?

A Party of One

Just as the gospel stories portray Jesus welcoming all kinds of people to his parties, invite the different parts of yourself to be part of your life. Identify the different parts of you (the good boy, the dutiful daughter, the trickster, the shy one, etc.) and make room in your inner life for each of them to have a voice.

It may be helpful to imagine yourself seated at a large table, and envision these different parts gathered at the table and given a voice.

Who is there?

Who sits next to whom?

What does each one want? (Or what desires or needs does each represent?)

What would you like to say to each one?

What would each one like to say to you?

Give your guests enough attention so their initial strangeness disappears and you recognize and understand the gifts they bear.

Notes

1. Cowabunga!

1. Alison Bonds Shapiro, "Trusting Each Other: What Is Trust Anyway?" in *Healing into Possibility: The Transformational Lessons of a Stroke* (Novato, CA: HJ Kramer / New World Library, 2009); www.psychologytoday.com/blog/healing-possibility/201204/trusting-each-other (accessed August 26, 2013).
2. David Richo, *Daring to Trust: Opening Ourselves to Real Love and Intimacy* (Boston: Shambhala, 2011), p. 14.
3. Marianne Williamson, "Trust Is Shorthand for Going with the Flow," *O, The Oprah Magazine* (December 2000); www.oprah.com/spirit/Marianne-Williamson-Trust-is-Shorthand-for-Going-With-the-Flow (accessed August 26, 2013).
4. Thomas P. McDonnell, *Through the Year with Thomas Merton* (New York: Galilee Trade, 1985), p. 4.
5. Joan Chittister, 2009 interview, *Top Spiritual Heroes*; www.topspiritualheroes.com/herojoan.html (accessed March 17, 2014).
6. David Whyte, *Crossing the Unknown Sea* (New York: Riverhead, 2002).

2. Humble Me

1. Parker J. Palmer, *A Hidden Wholeness: The Journey Toward an Undivided Life* (New York: John Wiley & Sons, Inc., 2009), p. 38.
2. Marianne Williamson, *A Return to Love: Reflections on the Principles of "A Course in Miracles"* (San Francisco: HarperOne, 1996).
3. Walter Burghardt, "Contemplation: A Long, Loving Look at the Real," *Church* 14 (Winter 1989): 15.
4. Richard Rohr, *Immortal Diamond: The Search for Our True Self* (San Francisco: Jossey-Bass, 2013), p. 27.
5. Sue Monk Kidd, *When the Heart Waits: Spiritual Direction for Life's Sacred Questions* (San Francisco: HarperOne, 2006), p. 55.
6. Robert C. Morris, "Meek as Moses: Humility, Self-Esteem, and the Service of God," *Weavings* (May/June 2000): 36–44.

7. Rainer Maria Rilke, *The Book of Hours: Prayers to a Lowly God* (New York: Penguin, 2005), p. 165.

3. A Burning Bush in Every Backyard

1. G. K. Chesterton, *Orthodoxy* (Chicago: Moody Publishers, 2009), pp. 4–5.
2. Abraham Joshua Heschel, *Who Is Man?* (Redwood City, CA: Stanford University Press, 1965), p. 89.
3. James Thornton, *A Field Guide to the Soul: A Down-to-Earth Handbook of Spiritual Practice* (New York: Harmony Books, 2000).
4. Kathleen Norris, *Amazing Grace: A Vocabulary of Faith* (New York: Penguin, 1999), p. 105.
5. Karl Rahner, *Karl Rahner im Gespräch* 1:1964–1977, ed. Paul Imhof and Hubert Billowons (Munich: Kösel Verlag, 1982), p. 301.
6. Gerald May, *Will and Spirit: A Contemplative Psychology* (San Francisco: HarperOne, 1987), p. 31.
7. Ibid., p. 25.
8. Norris, *Amazing Grace*, p. 351.

4. The Eyes of Innocence

1. Marguerite Wright, *I'm Chocolate, You're Vanilla: Raising Healthy Black and Biracial Children in a Race-Conscious World* (San Francisco: Jossey-Bass, 2000).
2. Dr. Gregg Henriques, "On Making Judgments and Being Judgmental," *Psychology Today*, May 17, 2013; www.psychologytoday.com/blog/theory-knowledge/201305/making-judgments-and-being-judgmental.
3. Bradley Shavit Artson, *God of Becoming and Relationship: The Dynamic Nature of Process Theology* (Woodstock, VT: Jewish Lights Publishing, 2013), p. 19.
4. Matthew Fox and Rupert Sheldrake, *Natural Grace: Dialogues on Creation, Darkness, and the Soul in Spirituality and Science* (New York: Image, 1997), p. 96.
5. Palmer, *A Hidden Wholeness*, p. 58.
6. https://community.pepperdine.edu/hr/current-employees/christmas2009.pdf (accessed January 12, 2014).

5. The Truth of a Tantrum

1. James Hillman, *The Soul's Code: In Search of Character and Calling* (New York: Grand Central, 1997), pp. 17–18.
2. Ann and Barry Ulanov, *Primary Speech: A Psychology of Prayer* (Louisville, KY: Westminster John Knox, 1983), pp. 1–2.

3. May, *Will and Spirit*, p. 214.
4. Martha Beck, "Four Steps to Find Your Life's Path," January 15, 2006, www.oprah.com/spirit/Your-Best-Life-Is-Waiting-by-Martha-Beck.
5. Ibid.
6. Philip Sheldrake, *Befriending Our Desires* (Eugene, OR: Wipf & Stock, 2012), p. 26.
7. Ulanov, *Primary Speech*, p. 8.
8. Ibid., p. 115.

6. Change the Way You Think

1. Irwin Kula, *Yearnings: Embracing the Sacred Messiness of Life* (New York: Hyperion, 2007), p. 61.
2. Patricia Hart Clifford, *Sitting Still: An Encounter with Christian Zen* (New York: Paulist Press, 1994), p. 75.
3. Edmond Jabés, *The Book of Questions* (Indianapolis: Wesleyan, 1991).
4. Richard Rohr, "Peace of Mind Is a Contradiction in Terms," daily email meditation, July 17, 2013.
5. Kula, *Yearnings*, p. 17.
6. Diane Ackerman, *Deep Play* (New York: Vintage, 2000), p. 20.
7. See www.integralinstitute.org for more information.

7. Let It Be and Let It Go

1. Lewis B. Smedes, *Forgive & Forget: Healing the Hurts We Don't Deserve* (San Francisco: HarperOne, 1996), excerpted by *Spirituality & Practice*, http://www.spiritualityandpractice.com/books/excerpts.php?id=14077 (accessed March 23, 2014).
2. Joan Chittister, *God's Tender Mercy: Reflections on Forgiveness* (New London, CT: Twenty-Third Publications, 2010), pp. 44–45.
3. Neil Rosenthal, "To Forgive Someone Who Hurt You, Here Are the Steps to Take," *Denver Post*, May 2, 2013.
4. Mark Twain, "The War Prayer" (1923).
5. Michael McCullough, "Getting Revenge and Forgiveness," *On Being*, American Public Media (May 24, 2012).
6. Zen Stories, http://goto.bilkent.edu.tr/gunes/ZEN/zenstories1.htm (accessed December 16, 2013).
7. Gerald May, *The Awakened Heart: Opening Yourself to the Love You Need* (San Francisco: HarperOne, 1991), pp. 234–235.
8. Hugh Prather, *Morning Notes: 365 Meditations to Wake You Up* (Newburyport, MA: Conari Press, 2005), p. 306.

8. Fully Embodied, Fully Inspirited

1. Artson, *God of Becoming and Relationships*, p. 19.
2. Thomas à Kempis, *The Imitation of Christ: Complete and Unabridged* (Peabody, MA: Hendrickson, 2011), p. 69.
3. Julian of Norwich, *Showings*, trans. Edmund Colledge and James Walsh (New York: Paulist Press, 1978), p. 186.
4. Frederic Luskin and Kenneth R. Pelletier, *Stress Free for Good: 10 Scientifically Proven Life Skills for Health and Happiness* (San Francisco: HarperOne, 2005), p. 156.
5. Megan MacArthur, "Why Dance?" September 13, 2011, www.meganmacarthur.wordpress.com/tag/nia.

9. Laughter and a Sense of Humor

1. "Philosophy of Humor," *Stanford Encyclopedia of Philosophy*, November 20, 2012; plato.stanford.edu/entries/humor.
2. Russell Grieger, www.psychologytoday.com/blog/happiness-purpose/201309/lighten-and-laugh (accessed March 24, 2014).
3. Susan Sparks, *Laugh Your Way to Grace: Reclaiming the Spiritual Power of Humor* (Woodstock, VT: SkyLight Paths, 2010), p. xv.
4. Chesterton, *Orthodoxy*, p. 223.
5. Katherine Mansfield, journal entry (October 1922), published in *The Journal of Katherine Mansfield*, ed. J. Middleton Murry (New York: A. A. Knopf, 1927).
6. Ethel Barrymore, quoted in John Hurley, *Before Your Dog Can Eat Your Homework, First You Have to Do It: Life Lessons from a Wise Old Dog to a Young Boy* (New York: Hudson Street Press, 2007), p. 121.
7. Sparks, *Laugh Your Way to Grace*, p. 79.
8. Grieger, www.psychologytoday.com/blog/happiness-purpose/201309/lighten-and-laugh.

10. Recess!

1. Ackerman, *Deep Play*, 1999, p. 4.
2. David Dobbs, "Playing for All Kinds of Possibilities," *New York Times*, April 22, 2013; www.nytimes.com/2013/04/23/science/zeal-for-play-may-have-propelled-human-evolution.html.
3. Dr. Alison Gopnik, quoted in Dobbs, "Playing for All Kinds of Possibilities."
4. Nina Quirk, "Play as a Spiritual Practice," February 24, 2010; www.examiner.com/article/play-as-a-spiritual-practice.
5. Plato, *Laws*, quoted in Ackerman, *Deep Play*, p. vii.
6. Ackerman, *Deep Play*, p. 106.

11. Inside Out, Outside In

1. Rohr, *Immortal Diamond*, p. 29.
2. Palmer, *A Hidden Wholeness*, p. 40.
3. Ibid.
4. Ibid., p. 45.
5. Ibid., p. 46.
6. Ibid., p. 47.
7. Paul Tillich, "You Are Accepted," in *The Shaking of the Foundations* (New York: Charles Scribner's Sons, 1953), pp. 161–162.
8. Thomas Moore, *Soul Mates: Honoring the Mysteries of Love and Relationship* (San Francisco: HarperOne, 1991), p. 42.
9. Donna Schaper, *Stripping Down: The Art of Spiritual Restoration* (San Diego: Lura Media, 1991), p. 8.
10. David Whyte, *The Heart Aroused: Poetry and the Preservation of the Soul in Corporate America* (New York: Doubleday, 1994), p. 69.

12. It Takes a Long Time to Become Young

1. Palmer, *A Hidden Wholeness*, pp. 32–33.
2. Thomas Moore, *Dark Nights of the Soul* (New York: Gotham Books, 2004), p. 197.
3. C. G. Jung, *Memories, Dreams, Reflections*, ed. Aniela Jaffe, trans. Richard and Clara Winston (New York: Pantheon Books, 1973), p. 174.
4. Timothy Shriver, "Beware of Pope Francis," February 13, 2014, www.faithstreet.com/onfaith/2014/02/13/beware-of-pope-francis/30949.
5. John O'Donohue, *Beauty: Rediscovering the True Sources of Compassion, Serenity, and Hope* (New York: HarperCollins, 2004), p. 173.
6. Ibid., p. 190.
7. Jueli Garfinkle, "The Holy Reb Zusya," in *Moon Over Maui: A Jewish Mystical Journey through the Year*, January, 26, 2012; roshchodeshnewmoon.com.

Suggestions for Further Reading

Akerman, Diane. *Deep Play*. New York: Vintage, 2000.

Artson, Bradley Shavit. *God of Becoming and Relationship: The Dynamic Nature of Process Theology*. Woodstock, VT: Jewish Lights Publishing, 2013.

Casey, Michael. *A Guide to Living in the Truth: Saint Benedict's Teaching on Humility*. Liguori, MO: Liguori, 2001.

Chesterton, G. K. *Orthodoxy*. Chicago: Moody Publishers, 2009.

Chittister, Joan. *God's Tender Mercy: Reflections on Forgiveness*. New London, CT: Twenty-Third Publications, 2010.

Clifford, Patricia Hart. *Sitting Still: An Encounter with Christian Zen*. Mahwah, NJ: Paulist Press, 1994.

Egan, Hope. *Holy Cow!: Does God Care about What We Eat?* Shelbyville, TN: Heart of Wisdom Publishing, 2012.

Fox, Matthew, and Rupert Sheldrake. *Natural Grace: Dialogues on Creation, Darkness, and the Soul in Spirituality and Science*. New York: Image, 1997.

Hillman, James. *The Soul's Code: In Search of Character and Calling*. New York: Grand Central, 1997.

Jabés, Edmond. *The Book of Questions*. Indianapolis: Wesleyan, 1991.

Jung, C. G. *Memories, Dreams, Reflections*. Edited by Aniela Jaffe, translated by Richard and Clara Winston. New York: Pantheon, 1973.

Kidd, Sue Monk. *Where the Heart Waits: Spiritual Direction for Life's Sacred Questions*. San Francisco: HarperOne, 2006.

Kula, Irwin. *Yearnings: Embracing the Sacred Messiness of Life*. New York: Hyperion, 2007.

Luskin, Frederic, and Kenneth R. Pelletier. *Stress Free for Good: 10 Scientifically Proven Life Skills for Health and Happiness*. San Francisco: HarperOne, 2005.

May, Gerald. *The Awakened Heart: Opening Yourself to the Love You Need*. San Francisco: HarperOne, 1993.

————. *Will and Spirit: A Contemplative Psychology*. San Francisco: HarperOne, 1987.

McDonnell, Thomas P. *Through the Year with Thomas Merton*. New York: Galilee Trade, 1985.

Moore, Thomas. *Dark Nights of the Soul: A Guide to Finding Your Way through Life's Ordeals*. New York: Gotham Books, 2004.

———. *Soul Mates: Honoring the Mystery of Love and Relationship*. San Francisco: Harper Perennial, 1994.

O'Donohue, John. *Beauty: Rediscovering the True Sources of Compassion, Serenity, and Hope*. New York: HarperCollins, 2004.

Palmer, Parker J. *A Hidden Wholeness: A Journey Toward an Undivided Life*. New York: John Wiley & Sons, 2004.

Prather, Hugh. *Morning Notes: 365 Meditations to Wake You Up*. Newburyport, MA: Conari Press, 2005.

Richo, David. *Daring to Trust: Opening Ourselves to Real Love and Intimacy*. Boston: Shambhala, 2011.

Rilke, Rainer Maria. *The Book of Hours: Prayers to a Lowly God*. Evanston, IL: Northwestern University Press, 2002.

Rohr, Richard. *Immortal Diamond: The Search for Our True Self*. San Francisco: Jossey-Bass, 2013.

Shapiro, Alison Bonds. *Healing into Possibility: The Transformational Lessons of a Stroke*. Novato, CA: HJ Kramer / New World Library, 2009.

Sheldrake, Philip. *Befriending Our Desires*. Eugene, OR: Wipf & Stock, 2012.

Smedes, Lewis B. *Forgive and Forget: Healing the Hurts We Don't Deserve*. San Francisco: HarperOne, 1996.

Sparks, Susan. *Laugh Your Way to Grace: Reclaiming the Spiritual Power of Humor*. Woodstock, VT: SkyLight Paths, 2010.

Thornton, James. *A Field Guide to the Soul: A Down-to-Earth Handbook of Spiritual Practice*. New York: Harmony Books, 2000.

Trueblood, Elton. *The Humor of Christ*. New York: Harper & Row, 1964.

Ulanov, Ann, and Barry Ulanov. *Primary Speech: A Psychology of Prayer*. Louisville, KY: Westminster John Knox, 1983.

Wallace, Peter. *The Passionate Jesus: What We Can Learn from Jesus about Love, Fear, Grief, Joy and Living Authentically*. Woodstock, VT: SkyLight Paths, 2012.

Whyte, David. *Crossing the Unknown Sea: Work as a Pilgrimage of Identity*. New York: Riverhead, 2002.

———. *The Heart Aroused: Poetry and the Preservation of the Soul in Corporate America*. New York: Crown, 1996.

Williamson, Marianne. *A Return to Love: Reflections on the Principles of "A Course in Miracles."* San Francisco: HarperOne, 1996.

Wright, Marguerite. *I'm Chocolate, You're Vanilla: Raising Healthy Black and Biracial Children in a Race-Conscious World*. San Francisco: Jossey-Bass, 2000.

Inspiration

The Rebirthing of God
Christianity's Struggle for New Beginnings
By John Philip Newell

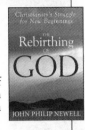

Drawing on modern prophets from East and West, and using the holy island of Iona as an icon of new beginnings, Celtic poet, peacemaker and scholar John Philip Newell dares us to imagine a new birth from deep within Christianity, a fresh stirring of the Spirit.
6 x 9, 150 pp (est), HC, 978-1-59473-542-4 **$19.99**

Finding God Beyond Religion: A Guide for Skeptics, Agnostics & Unorthodox Believers Inside & Outside the Church
By Tom Stella; Foreword by The Rev. Canon Marianne Wells Borg

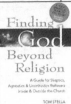

Reinterprets traditional religious teachings central to the Christian faith for people who have outgrown the beliefs and devotional practices that once made sense to them.
6 x 9, 160 pp, Quality PB, 978-1-59473-485-4 **$16.99**

Fully Awake and Truly Alive: Spiritual Practices to Nurture Your Soul
By Rev. Jane E. Vennard; Foreword by Rami Shapiro

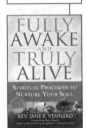

Illustrates the joys and frustrations of spiritual practice, offers insights from various religious traditions and provides exercises and meditations to help us become more fully alive.
6 x 9, 208 pp, Quality PB, 978-1-59473-473-1 **$16.99**

Journeys of Simplicity: Traveling Light with Thomas Merton, Bashō, Edward Abbey, Annie Dillard & Others *By Philip Harnden*

Invites you to consider a more graceful way of traveling through life. PB includes journal pages to help you get started on your own spiritual journey.
5 x 7¼, 144 pp, Quality PB, 978-1-59473-181-5 **$12.99**
5 x 7¼, 128 pp, HC, 978-1-893361-76-8 **$16.95**

Perennial Wisdom for the Spiritually Independent
Sacred Teachings—Annotated & Explained
Annotation by Rami Shapiro; Foreword by Richard Rohr
Weaves sacred texts and teachings from the world's major religions into a coherent exploration of the five core questions at the heart of every religion's search.
5½ x 8½, 336 pp, Quality PB Original, 978-1-59473-515-8 **$16.99**

Saving Civility: 52 Ways to Tame Rude, Crude & Attitude for a Polite Planet
By Sara Hacala

Provides fifty-two practical ways you can reverse the course of incivility and make the world a more enriching, pleasant place to live.
6 x 9, 240 pp, Quality PB, 978-1-59473-314-7 **$16.99**

Spiritually Healthy Divorce: Navigating Disruption with Insight & Hope
By Carolyne Call
A spiritual map to help you move through the twists and turns of divorce.
6 x 9, 224 pp, Quality PB, 978-1-59473-288-1 **$16.99**

Or phone, fax, mail or e-mail to: SKYLIGHT PATHS Publishing
Sunset Farm Offices, Route 4 • P.O. Box 237 • Woodstock, Vermont 05091
Tel: (802) 457-4000 • Fax: (802) 457-4004 • www.skylightpaths.com
Credit card orders: (800) 962-4544 (8:30AM–5:30PM EST Monday–Friday)
Generous discounts on quantity orders. SATISFACTION GUARANTEED. Prices subject to change.

Bible Stories / Folktales

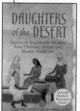

Abraham's Bind & Other Bible Tales of Trickery, Folly, Mercy and Love *By Michael J. Caduto*

New retellings of episodes in the lives of familiar biblical characters explore relevant life lessons. 6 x 9, 224 pp, HC, 978-1-59473-186-0 **$19.99**

Daughters of the Desert: Stories of Remarkable Women from Christian, Jewish and Muslim Traditions *By Claire Rudolf Murphy,*

Meghan Nuttall Sayres, Mary Cronk Farrell, Sarah Conover and Betsy Wharton

Breathes new life into the old tales of our female ancestors in faith. Uses traditional scriptural passages as starting points, then with vivid detail fills in historical context and place. Chapters reveal the voices of Sarah, Hagar, Huldah, Esther, Salome, Mary Magdalene, Lydia, Khadija, Fatima and many more. Historical fiction ideal for readers of all ages.

5½ x 8½, 192 pp, Quality PB, 978-1-59473-106-8 **$14.99** Inc. reader's discussion guide

The Triumph of Eve & Other Subversive Bible Tales
By Matt Biers-Ariel

These engaging retellings of familiar Bible stories are witty, often hilarious and always profound. They invite you to grapple with questions and issues that are often hidden in the original texts.

5½ x 8½, 192 pp, Quality PB, 978-1-59473-176-1 **$14.99**

Also available: **The Triumph of Eve Teacher's Guide**
8½ x 11, 44 pp, PB, 978-1-59473-152-5 **$8.99**

Wisdom in the Telling
Finding Inspiration and Grace in Traditional Folktales and Myths Retold
By Lorraine Hartin-Gelardi
6 x 9, 192 pp, HC, 978-1-59473-185-3 **$19.99**

Religious Etiquette / Reference

How to Be a Perfect Stranger, 5th Edition: The Essential Religious Etiquette Handbook *Edited by Stuart M. Matlins and Arthur J. Magida*

The indispensable guidebook to help the well-meaning guest when visiting other people's religious ceremonies. A straightforward guide to the rituals and celebrations of the major religions and denominations in the United States and Canada from the perspective of an interested guest of any other faith, based on information obtained from authorities of each religion. Belongs in every living room, library and office. Covers:

African American Methodist Churches • Assemblies of God • Bahá'í Faith • Baptist • Buddhist • Christian Church (Disciples of Christ) • Christian Science (Church of Christ, Scientist) • Churches of Christ • Episcopalian and Anglican • Hindu • Islam • Jehovah's Witnesses • Jewish • Lutheran • Mennonite/Amish • Methodist • Mormon (Church of Jesus Christ of Latter-day Saints) • Native American/First Nations • Orthodox Churches • Pentecostal Church of God • Presbyterian • Quaker (Religious Society of Friends) • Reformed Church in America/Canada • Roman Catholic • Seventh-day Adventist • Sikh • Unitarian Universalist • United Church of Canada • United Church of Christ

"The things Miss Manners forgot to tell us about religion."

—Los Angeles Times

"Finally, for those inclined to undertake their own spiritual journeys ... tells visitors what to expect." *—New York Times*

6 x 9, 432 pp, Quality PB, 978-1-59473-294-2 **$19.99**

The Perfect Stranger's Guide to Funerals and Grieving Practices: A Guide to Etiquette in Other People's Religious Ceremonies *Edited by Stuart M. Matlins*
6 x 9, 240 pp, Quality PB, 978-1-893361-20-1 **$16.95**

The Perfect Stranger's Guide to Wedding Ceremonies: A Guide to Etiquette in Other People's Religious Ceremonies *Edited by Stuart M. Matlins*
6 x 9, 208 pp, Quality PB, 978-1-893361-19-5 **$16.95**

Children's Spirituality

Remembering My Grandparent: A Kid's Own Grief Workbook in the Christian Tradition *By Nechama Liss-Levinson, PhD, and Rev. Molly Phinney Baskette, MDiv* 8 x 10, 48 pp, 2-color text, HC, 978-1-59473-212-6 **$16.99** *For ages 7 & up*

Does God Ever Sleep? *By Joan Sauro, CSJ*
A charming nighttime reminder that God is always present in our lives.
10 x 8½, 32 pp, Full-color photos, Quality PB, 978-1-59473-110-5 **$8.99** *For ages 3–6*

Does God Forgive Me? *By August Gold; Full-color photos by Diane Hardy Waller*
Gently shows how God forgives all that we do if we are truly sorry.
10 x 8½, 32 pp, Full-color photos, Quality PB, 978-1-59473-142-6 **$8.99** *For ages 3–6*

God Said Amen *By Sandy Eisenberg Sasso; Full-color illus. by Avi Katz*
A warm and inspiring tale that shows us that we need only reach out to each other to find the answers to our prayers.
9 x 12, 32 pp, Full-color illus., HC, 978-1-58023-080-3 **$16.95*** *For ages 4 & up*

How Does God Listen? *By Kay Lindahl; Full-color photos by Cynthia Maloney*
How do we know when God is listening to us? Children will find the answers to these questions as they engage their senses while the story unfolds, learning how God listens in the wind, waves, clouds, hot chocolate, perfume, our tears and our laughter.
10 x 8½, 32 pp, Full-color photos, Quality PB, 978-1-59473-084-9 **$8.99** *For ages 3–6*

In God's Hands *By Lawrence Kushner and Gary Schmidt; Full-color illus. by Matthew J. Baek*
A delightful, timeless legend that tells of the ordinary miracles that occur when we really, truly open our eyes to the world around us.
9 x 12, 32 pp, Full-color illus., HC, 978-1-58023-224-1 **$16.99*** *For ages 5 & up*

In God's Name *By Sandy Eisenberg Sasso; Full-color illus. by Phoebe Stone*
Like an ancient myth in its poetic text and vibrant illustrations, this award-winning modern fable about the search for God's name celebrates the diversity and, at the same time, the unity of all the people of the world.
9 x 12, 32 pp, Full-color illus., HC, 978-1-879045-26-2 **$16.99*** *For ages 4 & up*

Also available in Spanish: El nombre de Dios
9 x 12, 32 pp, Full-color illus., HC, 978-1-893361-63-8 **$16.95**

In Our Image: God's First Creatures
By Nancy Sohn Swartz; Full-color illus. by Melanie Hall
A playful new twist on the Genesis story—from the perspective of the animals. Celebrates the interconnectedness of nature and the harmony of all living things.
9 x 12, 32 pp, Full-color illus., HC, 978-1-879045-99-6 **$16.95*** *For ages 4 & up*
Animated app available on Apple App Store and the Google Play marketplace **$9.99**

Noah's Wife: The Story of Naamah
By Sandy Eisenberg Sasso; Full-color illus. by Bethanne Andersen
Opens young readers' religious imaginations to new ideas about the well-known story of the Flood. When God tells Noah to bring the animals of the world onto the ark, God also calls on Naamah, Noah's wife, to save each plant on Earth.
9 x 12, 32 pp, Full-color illus., HC, 978-1-58023-134-3 **$16.95*** *For ages 4 & up*

Also available: Naamah: Noah's Wife (A Board Book)
By Sandy Eisenberg Sasso; Full-color illus. by Bethanne Andersen
5 x 5, 24 pp, Full-color illus., Board Book, 978-1-893361-56-0 **$7.95** *For ages 1–4*

Where Does God Live? *By August Gold and Matthew J. Perlman*
Helps children and their parents find God in the world around us with simple, practical examples children can relate to.
10 x 8½, 32 pp, Full-color photos, Quality PB, 978-1-893361-39-3 **$8.99** *For ages 3–6*

*** A book from Jewish Lights, SkyLight Paths' sister imprint

Children's Spirituality—Board Books

Adam & Eve's New Day
By Sandy Eisenberg Sasso; Full-color illus. by Joani Keller Rothenberg
A lesson in hope for every child who has worried about what comes next. Abridged from *Adam & Eve's First Sunset*.
5 x 5, 24 pp, Full-color illus., Board Book, 978-1-59473-205-8 **$7.99** *For ages 1–4*

How Did the Animals Help God?
By Nancy Sohn Swartz; Full-color illus. by Melanie Hall
God asks all of nature to offer gifts to humankind—with a promise that they will care for creation in return. Abridged from *In Our Image*.
5 x 5, 24 pp, Full-color illus., Board Book, 978-1-59473-044-3 **$7.99** *For ages 1–4*

How Does God Make Things Happen?
By Lawrence and Karen Kushner; Full-color illus. by Dawn W. Majewski
A charming invitation for young children to explore how God makes things happen in our world. Abridged from *Because Nothing Looks Like God*.
5 x 5, 24 pp, Full-color illus., Board Book, 978-1-893361-24-9 **$7.95** *For ages 1–4*

What Does God Look Like?
By Lawrence and Karen Kushner; Full-color illus. by Dawn W. Majewski
A simple way for young children to explore the ways that we "see" God. Abridged from *Because Nothing Looks Like God*.
5 x 5, 24 pp, Full-color illus., Board Book, 978-1-893361-23-2 **$7.99** *For ages 1–4*

What Is God's Name?
By Sandy Eisenberg Sasso; Full-color illus. by Phoebe Stone
Everyone and everything in the world has a name. What is God's name? Abridged from the award-winning *In God's Name*.
5 x 5, 24 pp, Full-color illus., Board Book, 978-1-893361-10-2 **$7.99** *For ages 1–4*

Where Is God? By Lawrence and Karen Kushner; Full-color illus. by
Dawn W. Majewski A gentle way for young children to explore how God is with us every day, in every way. Abridged from *Because Nothing Looks Like God*.
5 x 5, 24 pp, Full-color illus., Board Book, 978-1-893361-17-1 **$7.99** *For ages 1–4*

What You Will See Inside ...

Fun-to-read books with vibrant full-color photos show children ages 6 and up the who, what, when, where, why and how of traditional houses of worship, liturgical celebrations and rituals of different world faiths, empowering them to respect and understand their own religious traditions—and those of their friends and neighbors.

What You Will See Inside a Catholic Church
By Rev. Michael Keane; Foreword by Robert J. Kealey, EdD
Full-color photos by Aaron Pepis
8½ x 10½, 32 pp, Full-color photos, HC, 978-1-893361-54-6 **$17.95**

Also available in Spanish: **Lo que se puede ver dentro de una iglesia católica**
8½ x 10½, 32 pp, Full-color photos, HC, 978-1-893361-66-9 **$16.95**

What You Will See Inside a Hindu Temple
By Mahendra Jani, PhD, and Vandana Jani, PhD; Full-color photos by Neirah Bhargava and Vijay Dave
8½ x 10½, 32 pp, Full-color photos, HC, 978-1-59473-116-7 **$17.99**

What You Will See Inside a Mosque
By Aisha Karen Khan; Full-color photos by Aaron Pepis
8½ x 10½, 32 pp, Full-color photos, Quality PB, 978-1-59473-257-7 **$8.99**

What You Will See Inside a Synagogue
By Rabbi Lawrence A. Hoffman, PhD, and Dr. Ron Wolfson; Full-color photos by Bill Aron
8½ x 10½, 32 pp, Full-color photos, Quality PB, 978-1-59473-256-0 **$8.99**

Children's Spiritual Biography

MULTICULTURAL, NONDENOMINATIONAL, NONSECTARIAN

Ten Amazing People
And How They Changed the World
By Maura D. Shaw; Foreword by Dr. Robert Coles
Full-color illus. by Stephen Marchesi

For ages 7 & up

Shows kids that spiritual people can have an exciting impact on the world around them. Kids will delight in reading about these amazing people and what they accomplished through their words and actions.

Black Elk • Dorothy Day • Malcolm X • Mahatma Gandhi • Martin Luther King, Jr. • Mother Teresa • Janusz Korczak • Desmond Tutu • Thich Nhat Hanh • Albert Schweitzer

"Best Juvenile/Young Adult Non-Fiction Book of the Year."
—*Independent Publisher*

"Will inspire adults and children alike."
—*Globe and Mail* (Toronto)

8½ x 11, 48 pp, Full-color illus., HC, 978-1-893361-47-8 **$17.95** *For ages 7 & up*

Spiritual Biographies for Young People
For Ages 7 & Up

By Maura D. Shaw; Illus. by Stephen Marchesi
6¾ x 8¾, 32 pp, Full-color and b/w illus., HC

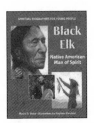 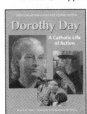 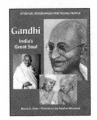 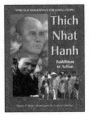

Black Elk: Native American Man of Spirit
Through historically accurate illustrations and photos, inspiring age-appropriate activities and Black Elk's own words, this colorful biography introduces children to a remarkable person who ensured that the traditions and beliefs of his people would not be forgotten.
978-1-59473-043-6 **$12.99**

Dorothy Day: A Catholic Life of Action
Introduces children to one of the most inspiring women of the twentieth century, a down-to-earth spiritual leader who saw the presence of God in every person she met. Includes practical activities, a timeline and a list of important words to know.
978-1-59473-011-5 **$12.99**

Gandhi: India's Great Soul
The only biography of Gandhi that balances a simple text with illustrations, photos and activities that encourage children and adults to talk about how to make changes happen without violence. Introduces children to important concepts of freedom, equality and justice among people of all backgrounds and religions.
978-1-893361-91-1 **$12.95**

Thich Nhat Hanh: Buddhism in Action
Warm illustrations, photos, age-appropriate activities and Thich Nhat Hanh's own poems introduce a great man to children in a way they can understand and enjoy. Includes a list of important Buddhist words to know.
978-1-893361-87-4 **$12.95**

Retirement and Later-Life Spirituality

Caresharing
A Reciprocal Approach to Caregiving and Care Receiving in the Complexities of Aging, Illness or Disability
By Marty Richards
Shows how to move from independent to *inter*dependent caregiving, so that the "cared for" and the "carer" share a deep sense of connection.
6 x 9, 256 pp, Quality PB, 978-1-59473-286-7 **$16.99**; HC, 978-1-59473-247-8 **$24.99**

How Did I Get to Be 70 When I'm 35 Inside?
Spiritual Surprises of Later Life
By Linda Douty
Encourages you to focus on the inner changes of aging to help you greet your later years as the grand adventure they can be.
6 x 9, 208 pp, Quality PB, 978-1-59473-297-3 **$16.99**

Soul Fire
Accessing Your Creativity
By Thomas Ryan, CSP
This inspiring guide shows you how to cultivate your creative spirit, particularly in the second half of life, as a way to encourage personal growth, enrich your spiritual life and deepen your communion with God.
6 x 9, 160 pp, Quality PB, 978-1-59473-243-0 **$16.99**

Restoring Life's Missing Pieces
The Spiritual Power of Remembering & Reuniting with People, Places, Things & Self
By Caren Goldman; Foreword by Dr. Nancy Copeland-Payton
Delve deeply into ways that your body, mind and spirit answer the Spirit of Re-union's calls to reconnect with people, places, things and self. A powerful and thought-provoking look at "reunions" of all kinds as roads to remembering the missing pieces of our stories, psyches and souls.
6 x 9, 208 pp, Quality PB, 978-1-59473-295-9 **$16.99**

Creative Aging
Rethinking Retirement and Non-Retirement in a Changing World
By Marjory Zoet Bankson
Explores the spiritual dimensions of retirement and aging and offers creative ways for you to share your gifts and experience, particularly when retirement leaves you questioning who you are when you are no longer defined by your career.
6 x 9, 160 pp, Quality PB, 978-1-59473-281-2 **$16.99**

Creating a Spiritual Retirement
A Guide to the Unseen Possibilities in Our Lives
By Molly Srode
Retirement can be an opportunity to refocus on your soul and deepen the presence of spirit in your life. With fresh spiritual reflections and questions to help you explore this new phase.
6 x 9, 208 pp, b/w photos, Quality PB, 978-1-59473-050-4 **$14.99**

Keeping Spiritual Balance as We Grow Older
More than 65 Creative Ways to Use Purpose, Prayer, and the Power of Spirit to Build a Meaningful Retirement
By Molly and Bernie Srode
As we face new demands on our bodies, it's easy to focus on the physical and forget about the transformations in our spiritual selves. This book is brimming with creative, practical ideas to add purpose and spirit to a meaningful retirement.
8 x 8, 224 pp, Quality PB, 978-1-59473-042-9 **$16.99**

Sacred Texts—SkyLight Illuminations Series

Offers today's spiritual seeker an enjoyable entry into the great classic texts of the world's spiritual traditions. Each classic is presented in an accessible translation, with facing pages of guided commentary from experts, giving you the keys you need to understand the history, context and meaning of the text.

CHRISTIANITY

The Book of Common Prayer: A Spiritual Treasure Chest—
Selections Annotated & Explained
Annotation by The Rev. Canon C. K. Robertson, PhD; Foreword by The Most Rev. Katharine Jefferts Schori; Preface by Archbishop Desmond Tutu
Makes available the riches of this spiritual treasure chest for all who are interested in deepening their life of prayer, building stronger relationships and making a difference in their world. 5½ x 8½. 208 pp, Quality PB Original, 978-1-59473-524-0 **$16.99**

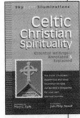

Celtic Christian Spirituality: Essential Writings—Annotated & Explained
Annotation by Mary C. Earle; Foreword by John Philip Newell
Explores how the writings of this lively tradition embody the gospel.
5½ x 8½, 176 pp, Quality PB, 978-1-59473-302-4 **$16.99**

Desert Fathers and Mothers: Early Christian Wisdom Sayings—
Annotated & Explained   *Annotation by Christine Valters Paintner, PhD*
Opens up wisdom of the desert fathers and mothers for readers with no previous knowledge of Western monasticism and early Christianity.
5½ x 8½, 192 pp, Quality PB, 978-1-59473-373-4 **$16.99**

The End of Days: Essential Selections from Apocalyptic Texts—
Annotated & Explained   *Annotation by Robert G. Clouse, PhD*
Helps you understand the complex Christian visions of the end of the world.
5½ x 8½, 224 pp, Quality PB, 978-1-59473-170-9 **$16.99**

The Hidden Gospel of Matthew: Annotated & Explained
Translation & Annotation by Ron Miller
Discover the words and events that have the strongest connection to the historical Jesus.
5½ x 8½, 272 pp, Quality PB, 978-1-59473-038-2 **$16.99**

The Imitation of Christ: Selections Annotated & Explained
Annotation by Paul Wesley Chilcote, PhD; By Thomas à Kempis; Adapted from John Wesley's The Christian's Pattern
Let Jesus's example of holiness, humility and purity of heart be a companion on your own spiritual journey.
5½ x 8½, 224 pp, Quality PB, 978-1-59473-434-2 **$16.99**

The Infancy Gospels of Jesus: Apocryphal Tales from the Childhoods of Mary and Jesus—Annotated & Explained
Translation & Annotation by Stevan Davies; Foreword by A. Edward Siecienski, PhD
A startling presentation of the early lives of Mary, Jesus and other biblical figures that will amuse and surprise you. 5½ x 8½, 176 pp, Quality PB, 978-1-59473-258-4 **$16.99**

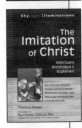

John & Charles Wesley: Selections from Their Writings and Hymns—
Annotated & Explained   *Annotation by Paul W. Chilcote, PhD*
A unique presentation of the writings of these two inspiring brothers brings together some of the most essential material from their large corpus of work.
5½ x 8½, 288 pp, Quality PB, 978-1-59473-309-3 **$16.99**

Julian of Norwich: Selections from *Revelations of Divine Love*—Annotated & Explained   *Annotation by Mary C. Earle*
Addresses topics including the infinite nature of God, the life of prayer, God's suffering with us, the eternal and undying life of the soul, the motherhood of Jesus and the motherhood of God and more.
5½ x 8½, 160 pp (est), Quality PB Original, 978-1-59473-513-4 **$16.99**

Sacred Texts—continued

CHRISTIANITY—continued

The Lost Sayings of Jesus: Teachings from Ancient Christian, Jewish, Gnostic and Islamic Sources—Annotated & Explained
Translation & Annotation by Andrew Phillip Smith; Foreword by Stephan A. Hoeller
Depicts Jesus as a Wisdom teacher who speaks to people of all faiths as a mystic and spiritual master. 5½ x 8½, 240 pp, Quality PB, 978-1-59473-172-3 **$16.99**

Philokalia: The Eastern Christian Spiritual Texts—Selections
Annotated & Explained *Annotation by Allyne Smith; Translation by G. E. H. Palmer, Phillip Sherrard and Bishop Kallistos Ware* The first approachable introduction to the wisdom of the Philokalia. 5½ x 8½, 240 pp, Quality PB, 978-1-59473-103-7 **$16.99**

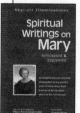

The Sacred Writings of Paul: Selections Annotated & Explained
Translation & Annotation by Ron Miller Leads you into the exciting immediacy of Paul's teachings. 5½ x 8½, 224 pp, Quality PB, 978-1-59473-213-3 **$16.99**

Saint Augustine of Hippo: Selections from *Confessions* and Other Essential Writings—Annotated & Explained
Annotation by Joseph T. Kelley, PhD; Translation by the Augustinian Heritage Institute
Provides insight into the mind and heart of this foundational Christian figure.
5½ x 8½, 272 pp, Quality PB, 978-1-59473-282-9 **$16.99**

Saint Ignatius Loyola—The Spiritual Writings: Selections
Annotated & Explained *Annotation by Mark Mossa, SJ* Focuses on the practical mysticism of Ignatius of Loyola. 5½ x 8½, 288 pp, Quality PB, 978-1-59473-301-7 **$16.99**

Sex Texts from the Bible: Selections Annotated & Explained
Translation & Annotation by Teresa J. Hornsby; Foreword by Amy-Jill Levine
Demystifies the Bible's ideas on gender roles, marriage, sexual orientation, virginity, lust and sexual pleasure. 5½ x 8½, 208 pp, Quality PB, 978-1-59473-217-1 **$16.99**

Spiritual Writings on Mary: Annotated & Explained
Annotation by Mary Ford-Grabowsky; Foreword by Andrew Harvey
Examines the role of Mary, the mother of Jesus, as a source of inspiration in history and in life today. 5½ x 8½, 288 pp, Quality PB, 978-1-59473-001-6 **$16.99**

The Way of a Pilgrim: The Jesus Prayer Journey—Annotated & Explained
Translation & Annotation by Gleb Pokrovsky; Foreword by Andrew Harvey A classic of Russian Orthodox spirituality. 5½ x 8½, 160 pp, Illus., Quality PB, 978-1-893361-31-7 **$14.95**

GNOSTICISM

Gnostic Writings on the Soul: Annotated & Explained
Translation & Annotation by Andrew Phillip Smith; Foreword by Stephan A. Hoeller
Reveals the inspiring ways your soul can remember and return to its unique, divine purpose. 5½ x 8½, 144 pp, Quality PB, 978-1-59473-220-1 **$16.99**

The Gospel of Philip: Annotated & Explained
Translation & Annotation by Andrew Phillip Smith; Foreword by Stevan Davies
Reveals otherwise unrecorded sayings of Jesus and fragments of Gnostic mythology.
5½ x 8½, 160 pp, Quality PB, 978-1-59473-111-2 **$16.99**

The Gospel of Thomas: Annotated & Explained
Translation & Annotation by Stevan Davies; Foreword by Andrew Harvey
Sheds new light on the origins of Christianity and portrays Jesus as a wisdom-loving sage.
5½ x 8½, 192 pp, Quality PB, 978-1-893361-45-4 **$16.99**

The Secret Book of John: The Gnostic Gospel—Annotated & Explained
Translation & Annotation by Stevan Davies The most significant and influential text of the ancient Gnostic religion. 5½ x 8½, 208 pp, Quality PB, 978-1-59473-082-5 **$16.99**

See Inspiration for *Perennial Wisdom for the Spiritually Independent: Sacred Teachings—Annotated & Explained*

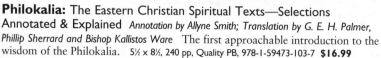

Spirituality / Animal Companions

Blessing the Animals
Prayers and Ceremonies to Celebrate God's Creatures, Wild and Tame
Edited and with Introductions by Lynn L. Caruso
5¼ x 7¼, 256 pp, Quality PB, 978-1-59473-253-9 **$15.99**; HC, 978-1-59473-145-7 **$19.99**

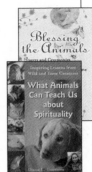

Remembering My Pet
A Kid's Own Spiritual Workbook for When a Pet Dies
By Nechama Liss-Levinson, PhD, and Rev. Molly Phinney Baskette, MDiv
Foreword by Lynn L. Caruso
8 x 10, 48 pp, 2-color text, HC, 978-1-59473-221-8 **$16.99**

What Animals Can Teach Us about Spirituality
Inspiring Lessons from Wild and Tame Creatures
By Diana L. Guerrero 6 x 9, 176 pp, Quality PB, 978-1-893361-84-3 **$16.95**

Spirituality & Crafts

Beading—The Creative Spirit
Finding Your Sacred Center through the Art of Beadwork
By Rev. Wendy Ellsworth
Invites you on a spiritual pilgrimage into the kaleidoscope world of glass and color.
7 x 9, 240 pp, 8-page color insert, 40+ b/w photos and 40 diagrams, Quality PB, 978-1-59473-267-6 **$18.99**

Contemplative Crochet
A Hands-On Guide for Interlocking Faith and Craft
By Cindy Crandall-Frazier; Foreword by Linda Skolnik
Illuminates the spiritual lessons you can learn through crocheting.
7 x 9, 208 pp, b/w photos, Quality PB, 978-1-59473-238-6 **$16.99**

The Knitting Way
A Guide to Spiritual Self-Discovery
By Linda Skolnik and Janice MacDaniels
Examines how you can explore and strengthen your spiritual life through knitting.
7 x 9, 240 pp, b/w photos, Quality PB, 978-1-59473-079-5 **$16.99**

The Painting Path
Embodying Spiritual Discovery through Yoga, Brush and Color
By Linda Novick; Foreword by Richard Segalman
Explores the divine connection you can experience through art.
7 x 9, 208 pp, 8-page color insert, plus b/w photos, Quality PB, 978-1-59473-226-3 **$18.99**

The Quilting Path
A Guide to Spiritual Discovery through Fabric, Thread and Kabbalah
By Louise Silk
Explores how to cultivate personal growth through quilt making.
7 x 9, 192 pp, b/w photos and illus., Quality PB, 978-1-59473-206-5 **$16.99**

The Scrapbooking Journey
A Hands-On Guide to Spiritual Discovery
By Cory Richardson-Lauve; Foreword by Stacy Julian
Reveals how this craft can become a practice used to deepen and shape your life.
7 x 9, 176 pp, 8-page color insert, plus b/w photos, Quality PB, 978-1-59473-216-4 **$18.99**

The Soulwork of Clay
A Hands-On Approach to Spirituality
By Marjory Zoet Bankson; Photos by Peter Bankson
Takes you through the seven-step process of making clay into a pot, drawing parallels at each stage to the process of spiritual growth.
7 x 9, 192 pp, b/w photos, Quality PB, 978-1-59473-249-2 **$16.99**

Spiritual Poetry—The Mystic Poets

Experience these mystic poets as you never have before. Each beautiful, compact book includes a brief introduction to the poet's time and place, a summary of the major themes of the poet's mysticism and religious tradition, essential selections from the poet's most important works, and an appreciative preface by a contemporary spiritual writer.

Hafiz
The Mystic Poets
Translated and with Notes by Gertrude Bell
Preface by Ibrahim Gamard
Hafiz is known throughout the world as Persia's greatest poet, with sales of his poems in Iran today only surpassed by those of the Qur'an itself. His probing and joyful verse speaks to people from all backgrounds who long to taste and feel divine love and experience harmony with all living things.
5 x 7¼, 144 pp, HC, 978-1-59473-009-2 **$16.99**

Hopkins
The Mystic Poets
Preface by Rev. Thomas Ryan, CSP
Gerard Manley Hopkins, Christian mystical poet, is beloved for his use of fresh language and startling metaphors to describe the world around him. Although his verse is lovely, beneath the surface lies a searching soul, wrestling with and yearning for God.
5 x 7¼, 112 pp, HC, 978-1-59473-010-8 **$16.99**

Tagore
The Mystic Poets
Preface by Swami Adiswarananda
Rabindranath Tagore is often considered the Shakespeare of modern India. A great mystic, Tagore was the teacher of W. B. Yeats and Robert Frost, the close friend of Albert Einstein and Mahatma Gandhi, and the winner of the Nobel Prize for Literature. This beautiful sampling of Tagore's two most important works, *The Gardener* and *Gitanjali,* offers a glimpse into his spiritual vision that has inspired people around the world.
5 x 7¼, 144 pp, HC, 978-1-59473-008-5 **$16.99**

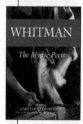

Whitman
The Mystic Poets
Preface by Gary David Comstock
Walt Whitman was the most innovative and influential poet of the nineteenth century. This beautiful sampling of Whitman's most important poetry from *Leaves of Grass,* and selections from his prose writings, offers a glimpse into the spiritual side of his most radical themes—love for country, love for others and love of self.
5 x 7¼, 192 pp, HC, 978-1-59473-041-2 **$16.99**

Spiritual Practice—The Sacred Art of Living Series

Dreaming—The Sacred Art: Incubating, Navigating & Interpreting Sacred Dreams for Spiritual & Personal Growth
By Lori Joan Swick
This fascinating introduction to sacred dreams celebrates the dream experience as a way to deepen spiritual awareness and as a source of self-healing. Designed for the novice and the experienced sacred dreamer of all faith traditions, or none.
5½ x 8½, 224 pp, Quality PB, 978-1-59473-544-8 **$16.99**

Conversation—The Sacred Art: Practicing Presence in an Age of Distraction
By Diane M. Millis, PhD; Foreword by Rev. Tilden Edwards, PhD
5½ x 8½, 192 pp, Quality PB, 978-1-59473-474-8 **$16.99**

Dance—The Sacred Art: The Joy of Movement as a Spiritual Practice
By Cynthia Winton-Henry 5½ x 8½, 224 pp, Quality PB, 978-1-59473-268-3 **$16.99**

Fly-Fishing—The Sacred Art: Casting a Fly as a Spiritual Practice
By Rabbi Eric Eisenkramer and Rev. Michael Attas, MD; Foreword by Chris Wood, CEO, Trout Unlimited; Preface by Lori Simon, executive director, Casting for Recovery
5½ x 8½, 160 pp, Quality PB, 978-1-59473-299-7 **$16.99**

Giving—The Sacred Art: Creating a Lifestyle of Generosity
By Lauren Tyler Wright 5½ x 8½, 208 pp, Quality PB, 978-1-59473-224-9 **$16.99**

Haiku—The Sacred Art: A Spiritual Practice in Three Lines
By Margaret D. McGee 5½ x 8½, 192 pp, Quality PB, 978-1-59473-269-0 **$16.99**

Hospitality—The Sacred Art: Discovering the Hidden Spiritual Power of Invitation and Welcome *By Rev. Nanette Sawyer; Foreword by Rev. Dirk Ficca*
5½ x 8½, 208 pp, Quality PB, 978-1-59473-228-7 **$16.99**

Labyrinths from the Outside In, 2nd Edition: Walking to Spiritual Insight—A Beginner's Guide *By Rev. Dr. Donna Schaper and Rev. Dr. Carole Ann Camp*
6 x 9, 208 pp, b/w illus. and photos, Quality PB, 978-1-59473-486-1 **$16.99**

Lectio Divina—**The Sacred Art**
Transforming Words & Images into Heart-Centered Prayer
By Christine Valters Paintner, PhD 5½ x 8½, 240 pp, Quality PB, 978-1-59473-300-0 **$16.99**

Pilgrimage—The Sacred Art: Journey to the Center of the Heart
By Dr. Sheryl A. Kujawa-Holbrook 5½ x 8½, 240 pp, Quality PB, 978-1-59473-472-4 **$16.99**

Practicing the Sacred Art of Listening: A Guide to Enrich Your Relationships and Kindle Your Spiritual Life *By Kay Lindahl* 8 x 8, 176 pp, Quality PB, 978-1-893361-85-0 **$18.99**

Recovery—The Sacred Art: The Twelve Steps as Spiritual Practice *by Rami Shapiro; Foreword by Joan Borysenko, PhD* 5½ x 8½, 240 pp, Quality PB, 978-1-59473-259-1 **$16.99**

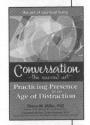

Running—The Sacred Art: Preparing to Practice *By Dr. Warren A. Kay; Foreword by Kristin Armstrong* 5½ x 8½, 160 pp, Quality PB, 978-1-59473-227-0 **$16.99**

The Sacred Art of Chant: Preparing to Practice
By Ana Hernández 5½ x 8½, 192 pp, Quality PB, 978-1-59473-036-8 **$16.99**

The Sacred Art of Fasting: Preparing to Practice
By Thomas Ryan, CSP 5½ x 8½, 192 pp, Quality PB, 978-1-59473-078-8 **$15.99**

The Sacred Art of Forgiveness: Forgiving Ourselves and Others through God's Grace
By Marcia Ford 8 x 8, 176 pp, Quality PB, 978-1-59473-175-4 **$18.99**

The Sacred Art of Listening: Forty Reflections for Cultivating a Spiritual Practice
By Kay Lindahl; Illus. by Amy Schnapper 8 x 8, 160 pp, b/w illus., Quality PB, 978-1-893361-44-7 **$16.99**

The Sacred Art of Lovingkindness: Preparing to Practice
By Rabbi Rami Shapiro; Foreword by Marcia Ford 5½ x 8½, 176 pp, Quality PB, 978-1-59473-151-8 **$16.99**

Thanking & Blessing—The Sacred Art: Spiritual Vitality through Gratefulness
By Jay Marshall, PhD; Foreword by Philip Gulley 5½ x 8½, 176 pp, Quality PB, 978-1-59473-231-7 **$16.99**

Writing—The Sacred Art: Beyond the Page to Spiritual Practice
By Rami Shapiro and Aaron Shapiro 5½ x 8½, 192 pp, Quality PB, 978-1-59473-372-7 **$16.99**

Spirituality

Like a Child
Restoring the Awe, Wonder, Joy and Resiliency of the Human Spirit
By Rev. Timothy J. Mooney

By breaking free from our misperceptions about what it means to be an adult, we can reshape our world and become harbingers of grace. This unique spiritual resource explores Jesus's counsel to become like children in order to enter the kingdom of God. 6 x 9, 144 pp (est), Quality PB, 978-1-59473-543-1 **$16.99**

The Passionate Jesus: What We Can Learn from Jesus about Love, Fear, Grief, Joy and Living Authentically
By The Rev. Peter Wallace

Reveals Jesus as a passionate figure who was involved, present, connected, honest and direct with others and encourages you to build personal authenticity in every area of your own life. 6 x 9, 208 pp, Quality PB, 978-1-59473-393-2 **$18.99**

Gathering at God's Table: The Meaning of Mission in the Feast of Faith
By Katharine Jefferts Schori

A profound reminder of our role in the larger frame of God's dream for a restored and reconciled world. 6 x 9, 256 pp, HC, 978-1-59473-316-1 **$21.99**

The Heartbeat of God: Finding the Sacred in the Middle of Everything
By Katharine Jefferts Schori; Foreword by Joan Chittister, OSB

Explores our connections to other people, to other nations and with the environment through the lens of faith.
6 x 9, 240 pp, HC, 978-1-59473-292-8 **$21.99**

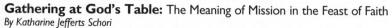

A Dangerous Dozen: Twelve Christians Who Threatened the Status Quo but Taught Us to Live Like Jesus
By the Rev. Canon C. K. Robertson, PhD; Foreword by Archbishop Desmond Tutu

Profiles twelve visionary men and women who challenged society and showed the world a different way of living.
6 x 9, 208 pp, Quality PB, 978-1-59473-298-0 **$16.99**

Laugh Your Way to Grace: Reclaiming the Spiritual Power of Humor
By Rev. Susan Sparks

A powerful, humorous case for laughter as a spiritual, healing path.
6 x 9, 176 pp, Quality PB, 978-1-59473-280-5 **$16.99**

Claiming Earth as Common Ground: The Ecological Crisis through the Lens of Faith
By Andrea Cohen-Kiener; Foreword by Rev. Sally Bingham
6 x 9, 192 pp, Quality PB, 978-1-59473-261-4 **$16.99**

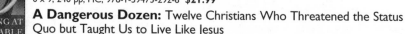

Living into Hope: A Call to Spiritual Action for Such a Time as This
By Rev. Dr. Joan Brown Campbell; Foreword by Karen Armstrong
6 x 9, 208 pp, Quality PB, 978-1-59473-436-6 $18.99; HC, 978-1-59473-283-6 **$21.99**

Renewal in the Wilderness
A Spiritual Guide to Connecting with God in the Natural World
By John Lionberger 6 x 9, 176 pp, b/w photos, Quality PB, 978-1-59473-219-5 **$16.99**

Spiritual Adventures in the Snow
Skiing & Snowboarding as Renewal for Your Soul
By Dr. Marcia McFee and Rev. Karen Foster; Foreword by Paul Arthur
5½ x 8½, 208 pp, Quality PB, 978-1-59473-270-6 **$8.50**

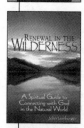

A Walk with Four Spiritual Guides: Krishna, Buddha, Jesus, and Ramakrishna
By Andrew Harvey 5½ x 8½ 192 pp, b/w photos & illus., Quality PB, 978-1-59473-138-9 **$15.99**

Who Is My God? 2nd Edition: An Innovative Guide to Finding Your Spiritual Identity
By the Editors at SkyLight Paths

Provides the Spiritual Identity Self-Test™ to uncover the components of your unique spirituality.
6 x 9, 160 pp, Quality PB, 978-1-59473-014-6 **$15.99**

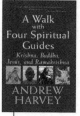

Prayer / Meditation

Openings, 2nd Edition
A Daybook of Saints, Sages, Psalms and Prayer Practices
By Rev. Larry J. Peacock
For anyone hungry for a richer prayer life, this prayer book offers daily inspiration to help you move closer to God. Draws on a wide variety of resources—lives of saints and sages from every age, psalms, and suggestions for personal reflection and practice. 6 x 9, 448 pp, Quality PB, 978-1-59473-545-5 **$18.99**

Men Pray: Voices of Strength, Faith, Healing, Hope and Courage
Created by the Editors at SkyLight Paths
Celebrates the rich variety of ways men around the world have called out to the Divine—with words of joy, praise, gratitude, wonder, petition and even anger—from the ancient world up to our own day.
5 x 7¼, 192 pp, HC, 978-1-59473-395-6 **$16.99**

Honest to God Prayer
Spirituality as Awareness, Empowerment, Relinquishment and Paradox
By Kent Ira Groff
For those turned off by shopworn religious language, offers innovative ways to pray based on both Native American traditions and Ignatian spirituality.
6 x 9, 192 pp, Quality PB, 978-1-59473-433-5 **$16.99**

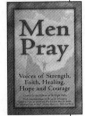

Sacred Attention: A Spiritual Practice for Finding God in the Moment
By Margaret D. McGee
Framed on the Christian liturgical year, this inspiring guide explores ways to develop a practice of attention as a means of talking—and listening—to God.
6 x 9, 144 pp, Quality PB, 978-1-59473-291-1 **$16.99**

Praying with Our Hands: 21 Practices of Embodied Prayer from the World's
Spiritual Traditions *By Jon M. Sweeney; Photos by Jennifer J. Wilson; Foreword by Mother Tessa Bielecki; Afterword by Taitetsu Unno, PhD*
8 x 8, 96 pp, 22 duotone photos, Quality PB, 978-1-893361-16-4 **$16.95**

Secrets of Prayer: A Multifaith Guide to Creating Personal Prayer in Your Life
By Nancy Corcoran, CSJ
6 x 9, 160 pp, Quality PB, 978-1-59473-215-7 **$16.99**

Three Gates to Meditation Practice: A Personal Journey into Sufism, Buddhism,
and Judaism *By David A. Cooper* 5½ x 8½, 240 pp, Quality PB, 978-1-893361-22-5 **$18.99**

Women of Color Pray: Voices of Strength, Faith, Healing, Hope and Courage
Edited and with Introductions by Christal M. Jackson
5 x 7¼, 208 pp, Quality PB, 978-1-59473-077-1 **$15.99**

Prayer / M. Basil Pennington, OCSO

Finding Grace at the Center, 3rd Edition: The Beginning of
Centering Prayer *With Thomas Keating, OCSO, and Thomas E. Clarke, SJ; Foreword by Rev. Cynthia Bourgeault, PhD* A practical guide to a simple and beautiful form of meditative prayer. 5 x 7¼,128 pp, Quality PB, 978-1-59473-182-2 **$12.99**

The Monks of Mount Athos: A Western Monk's Extraordinary
Spiritual Journey on Eastern Holy Ground *Foreword by Archimandrite Dionysios*
Explores the landscape, monastic communities and food of Athos.
6 x 9, 352 pp, Quality PB, 978-1-893361-78-2 **$18.95**

Psalms: A Spiritual Commentary *Illus. by Phillip Ratner*
Reflections on some of the most beloved passages from the Bible's most widely read book. 6 x 9, 176 pp, 24 full-page b/w illus., Quality PB, 978-1-59473-234-8 **$16.99**

The Song of Songs: A Spiritual Commentary *Illus. by Phillip Ratner*
Explore the Bible's most challenging mystical text.
6 x 9, 160 pp, 14 full-page b/w illus., Quality PB, 978-1-59473-235-5 **$16.99**
HC, 978-1-59473-004-7 **$19.99**

Women's Interest

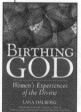

Birthing God: Women's Experiences of the Divine
By Lana Dalberg; Foreword by Kathe Schaaf
Powerful narratives of suffering, love and hope that inspire both personal and collective transformation. 6 x 9, 304 pp, Quality PB, 978-1-59473-480-9 **$18.99**

On the Chocolate Trail: A Delicious Adventure Connecting Jews, Religions, History, Travel, Rituals and Recipes to the Magic of Cacao
By Rabbi Deborah R. Prinz
Take a delectable journey through the religious history of chocolate—a real treat!
6 x 9, 272 pp, 20+ b/w photographs, Quality PB, 978-1-58023-487-0 **$18.99***

Women, Spirituality and Transformative Leadership
Where Grace Meets Power
Edited by Kathe Schaaf, Kay Lindahl, Kathleen S. Hurty, PhD, and Reverend Guo Cheen
A dynamic conversation on the power of women's spiritual leadership and its emerging patterns of transformation.
6 x 9, 288 pp, Quality PB, 978-1-59473-548-6 **$18.99**; HC, 978-1-59473-313-0 **$24.99**

Spiritually Healthy Divorce: Navigating Disruption with Insight & Hope
By Carolyne Call A spiritual map to help you move through the twists and turns of divorce. 6 x 9, 224 pp, Quality PB, 978-1-59473-288-1 **$16.99**

New Feminist Christianity: Many Voices, Many Views
Edited by Mary E. Hunt and Diann L. Neu
Insights from ministers and theologians, activists and leaders, artists and liturgists offer a starting point for building new models of religious life and worship.
6 x 9, 384 pp, Quality PB, 978-1-59473-435-9 **$19.99**; HC, 978-1-59473-285-0 **$24.99**

Bread, Body, Spirit: Finding the Sacred in Food
Edited and with Introductions by Alice Peck 6 x 9, 224 pp, Quality PB, 978-1-59473-242-3 **$19.99**

Dance—The Sacred Art: The Joy of Movement as a Spiritual Practice
By Cynthia Winton-Henry 5½ x 8½, 224 pp, Quality PB, 978-1-59473-268-3 **$16.99**

Daughters of the Desert: Stories of Remarkable Women from Christian, Jewish and Muslim Traditions
By Claire Rudolf Murphy, Meghan Nuttall Sayres, Mary Cronk Farrell, Sarah Conover and Betsy Wharton
5½ x 8½, 192 pp, Illus., Quality PB, 978-1-59473-106-8 **$14.99** Inc. reader's discussion guide

The Divine Feminine in Biblical Wisdom Literature
Selections Annotated & Explained
Translation & Annotation by Rabbi Rami Shapiro; Foreword by Rev. Cynthia Bourgeault, PhD
5½ x 8½, 240 pp, Quality PB, 978-1-59473-109-9 **$16.99**

Divining the Body: Reclaim the Holiness of Your Physical Self
By Jan Phillips 8 x 8, 256 pp, Quality PB, 978-1-59473-080-1 **$18.99**

Honoring Motherhood: Prayers, Ceremonies & Blessings
Edited and with Introductions by Lynn L. Caruso
5 x 7¼, 272 pp, Quality PB, 978-1-58473-384-0 **$9.99**; HC, 978-1-59473-239-3 **$19.99**

Next to Godliness: Finding the Sacred in Housekeeping
Edited by Alice Peck 6 x 9, 224 pp, Quality PB, 978-1-59473-214-0 **$19.99**

ReVisions: Seeing Torah through a Feminist Lens
By Rabbi Elyse Goldstein 5½ x 8½, 224 pp, Quality PB, 978-1-58023-117-6 **$16.95***

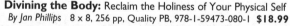

The Triumph of Eve & Other Subversive Bible Tales
By Matt Biers-Ariel 5½ x 8½, 192 pp, Quality PB, 978-1-59473-176-1 **$14.99**

White Fire: A Portrait of Women Spiritual Leaders in America
By Malka Drucker; Photos by Gay Block 7 x 10, 320 pp, b/w photos, HC, 978-1-893361-64-5 **$24.95**

Woman Spirit Awakening in Nature: Growing Into the Fullness of Who You Are
By Nancy Barrett Chickerneo, PhD; Foreword by Eileen Fisher
8 x 8, 224 pp, b/w illus., Quality PB, 978-1-59473-250-8 **$16.99**

Women of Color Pray: Voices of Strength, Faith, Healing, Hope and Courage
Edited and with Introductions by Christal M. Jackson
5 x 7¼, 208 pp, Quality PB, 978-1-59473-077-1 **$15.99**

* A book from Jewish Lights, SkyLight Paths' sister imprint

Personal Growth

Decision Making & Spiritual Discernment
The Sacred Art of Finding Your Way
By Nancy L. Bieber

Presents three essential aspects of Spirit-led decision making: willingness, attentiveness and responsiveness.

5½ x 8½, 208 pp, Quality PB, 978-1-59473-289-8 **$16.99**

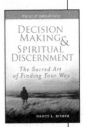

Like a Child
Restoring the Awe, Wonder, Joy and Resiliency of the Human Spirit
By Rev. Timothy J. Mooney

By breaking free from our misperceptions about what it means to be an adult, we can reshape our world and become harbingers of grace. This unique spiritual resource explores Jesus's counsel to become like children in order to enter the kingdom of God.

6 x 9, 144 pp (est), Quality PB, 978-1-59473-543-1 **$16.99**

Secrets of a Soulful Marriage
Creating & Sustaining a Loving, Sacred Relationship
By Jim Sharon, EdD, and Ruth Sharon, MS

An innovative, hope-filled resource for developing soulful, mature love for committed couples who are looking to create, maintain and glorify the sacred in their relationship. Offers a banquet of practical tools, inspirational real-life stories and spiritual practices for couples of all faiths, or none.

6 x 9, 200 pp (est), Quality PB, 978-1-59473-554-7 **$16.99**

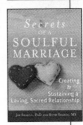

Conversation—The Sacred Art
Practicing Presence in an Age of Distraction
By Diane M. Millis, PhD; Foreword by Rev. Tilden Edwards, PhD

Cultivate the potential for deeper connection in every conversation.

5½ x 8½, 192 pp, Quality PB, 978-1-59473-474-8 **$16.99**

Hospitality—The Sacred Art
Discovering the Hidden Spiritual Power of Invitation and Welcome
By Rev. Nanette Sawyer; Foreword by Rev. Dirk Ficca

Discover how the qualities of hospitality can deepen your self-understanding and help you build transforming and lasting relationships with others and with God.

5½ x 8½, 208 pp, Quality PB, 978-1-59473-228-7 **$16.99**

The Losses of Our Lives
The Sacred Gifts of Renewal in Everyday Loss
By Dr. Nancy Copeland-Payton

Shows us that by becoming aware of what our lesser losses have to teach us, the larger losses become less terrifying. Includes spiritual practices and questions for reflection.

6 x 9, 192 pp, Quality PB, 978-1-59473-307-9 **$16.99**; HC, 978-1-59473-271-3 **$19.99**

A Spirituality for Brokenness
Discovering Your Deepest Self in Difficult Times
By Terry Taylor

Compassionately guides you through the practicalities of facing and finally accepting brokenness in your life—a process that can ultimately bring mending.

6 x 9, 176 pp, Quality PB, 978-1-59473-229-4 **$16.99**

The Bridge to Forgiveness
Stories and Prayers for Finding God and Restoring Wholeness
By Karyn D. Kedar

This inspiring guide for healing and wholeness supplies you with a map to help you along your forgiveness journey. Deeply personal stories, comforting prayers and intimate meditations gently lead you through the steps that allow the heart to forgive.

6 x 9, 176 pp, Quality PB, 978-1-58023-451-1 **$16.99***

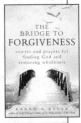

* A book from Jewish Lights, SkyLight Paths' sister imprint

About SKYLIGHT PATHS Publishing

SkyLight Paths Publishing is creating a place where people of different spiritual traditions come together for challenge and inspiration, a place where we can help each other understand the mystery that lies at the heart of our existence.

Through spirituality, our religious beliefs are increasingly becoming a part of our lives—rather than *apart* from our lives. While many of us may be more interested than ever in spiritual growth, we may be less firmly planted in traditional religion. Yet, we do want to deepen our relationship to the sacred, to learn from our own as well as from other faith traditions, and to practice in new ways.

SkyLight Paths sees both believers and seekers as a community that increasingly transcends traditional boundaries of religion and denomination—people wanting to learn from each other, *walking together, finding the way.*

For your information and convenience, at the back of this book we have provided a list of other SkyLight Paths books you might find interesting and useful. They cover the following subjects:

Buddhism / Zen	Gnosticism	Poetry
Catholicism	Hinduism / Vedanta	Prayer
Chaplaincy		Religious Etiquette
Children's Books	Inspiration	Retirement & Later-Life Spirituality
Christianity	Islam / Sufism	
Comparative Religion	Judaism	Spiritual Biography
	Meditation	Spiritual Direction
Earth-Based Spirituality	Mindfulness	Spirituality
	Monasticism	Women's Interest
Enneagram	Mysticism	Worship
Global Spiritual Perspectives	Personal Growth	

Or phone, fax, mail or e-mail to: SKYLIGHT PATHS Publishing
Sunset Farm Offices, Route 4 • P.O. Box 237 • Woodstock, Vermont 05091
Tel: (802) 457-4000 • Fax: (802) 457-4004 • www.skylightpaths.com
Credit card orders: (800) 962-4544 (8:30AM–5:30PM EST Monday–Friday)
Generous discounts on quantity orders. SATISFACTION GUARANTEED. Prices subject to change.

**For more information about each book,
visit our website at www.skylightpaths.com**